NEW
PRESSED FLOWER
DESIGNS

Alison Morris

NEW
PRESSED FLOWER
DESIGNS

ALISON MORRIS

MEREHURST

For Ian, with my thanks for his special support and love,
and to my mother, who passes to me her love of flowers

First published in 1997 by Merehurst Limited
Ferry House, 51-57 Lacy Road, Putney, London SW15 1PR
Photography and illustrations copyright © Merehurst 1997 except
for pages 6 and 8–10
Text copyright © Alison Morris 1997

ISBN 1 85391 548 3

A catalogue record for this book is available from the British
Library.

Edited by Heather Dewhurst

Designed by Sara Kidd

All photography by Caroline Arber, except for the following which
were supplied by The Garden Picture Library: page 6 by
B. Challinor, page 9 by P.W. Flowers, and page 10 by K. Charlton

Styling by Jane Cudlipp

Artwork by King & King Design Associates

Colour separation by Bright Arts (HK) Ltd.

Printed in Singapore by Tien Wah Press

CONTENTS

ꓕNTRODUCTION

It is only in recent years that I have begun to work with pressed flowers, but I have always had a great love of all flowers and worked as a florist for several years. With such a vast selection of plant material suitable for pressing, I had thought for a long time that there was tremendous scope for creative designs which moved away from the more traditional forms of pressed flower pictures.

My husband made my first small flower press as a gift and for some time I enjoyed the hobby of collecting flowers from our cottage garden and pressing them, with varying degrees of success. This stock of pressed flowers grew as I struggled for inspiration on what to do with them all. This came at last when we visited the stunning gardens of Villandry in France. Here, intricate parterre and knot garden designs were beautifully planted with fruit, flowers and vegetables. I returned home to experiment with my first picture, a reproduction of the 'tender love' knot garden at Villandry. Nowadays I continue to experiment with pressed plant material, gaining inspiration from many sources including garden designs, stitched samplers, fabric and interior design trends.

This book contains 25 pressed flower projects, all of which are clearly illustrated with step-by-step photographs. The projects are very different in style to help show the extraordinary versatility and range of pressed flowers. Some of the projects incorporate other popular crafts, such as papier mâché and stencilling. There are details of how to select and gather plant materials for pressing from different sources, such as the garden, the hedgerow and the seaside. The comprehensive section on pressing techniques details different methods of pressing, ranging from using a traditional flower press to the modern method of microwaving. It also includes techniques for pressing unusual materials, such as vegetables, fungi, seaweed and fruit.

With such a huge range of colours offered to us by flowers, any of the projects in this book could be altered to suit individual interiors. To assist in this, I have categorized plant material into colour bands, detailing how to press them and giving the colour when pressed.

I hope that this fresh approach to a traditional craft will encourage you to try the art of pressing flowers for yourself.

Right: A knot garden design using pressed herbs.

Below: The inspirational gardens of Villandry, France.

Choosing and Gathering Material for Pressing

The craft of flower pressing can be enjoyed by everyone. No matter where you live,
it is possible to find a large selection of plant material you can use.

A small garden can provide a good variety of annuals, perennials and shrubs. If space is limited, annuals can be grown in pots or baskets and can provide many wonderful flowers for pressing; lobelia, geranium, pansy and nigella are a few of my favourites. Perennials offer a floral display year after year and can be harvested for pressing in the summer months; delphinium, penstemon and lady's-mantle are a few I would not be without. It is always a good idea to press a selection of foliage too, as this provides the basis for most pressed flower designs. Shrubs provide an invaluable source of foliage, with an endless range of colour, shape and texture. A window box filled with herbs can yield a lot of material for pressing, particularly thyme, chives, rosemary and sage. An added bonus when pressing herbs is that they still retain their lovely strong scent.

Not all pressing material is gathered in the garden. A good florist can provide a great selection of fresh flowers suitable for pressing, from spring bulbs through to the more exotic blooms now widely available. A walk in the countryside is an ideal opportunity to gather a vast selection of plant material from many different habitats. Hedgerows produce a wealth of berries and seedheads throughout autumn and winter, while in the spring and summer months blossom and flowers are abundant. Gathering woodland flora can

Many garden flowers are suitable for pressing.

also provide a varied collection of material, from autumn leaves to fungi, bark and moss. Along the banks of streams and rivers, sedges and ferns can be collected, while in meadows, many grasses and wild flowers abound.

The availability of all these flowers and foliage throughout the year opens the world of pressed flowers to everyone.

COLLECTING WILD FLOWERS

Collecting flowers from the wild can provide a great source of material for pressing, but it is vital for the conservation of our wild flora that this is carried out in a responsible manner. When collecting from the wild take only a few flowers of any one species; gathering more than you need is a pointless waste of these precious flowers. Never pick a solitary bloom; instead leave it to grow to give the plant the best opportunity of seeding naturally. You should also never dig up any wild plants. When collecting from the countryside take a book on wild flowers with you for reference. This will help you to recognize all flora before it is collected for pressing.

Most of the wild flowers used in this book are grown in my garden. If you have none, why not try growing some from seed. Packets of wildflower seed are now widely available in garden centres and nurseries.

CHOOSING FLOWERS AND FOLIAGE

When choosing flowers for pressing, it is important to pick the blooms at their peak of freshness. The ideal time is just after the flower has fully opened. Do not be tempted to leave the flowers for a few days before

There is an official list of protected plants which should never be touched to protect their future development. This list is available from:

The Department of Environment,
European Wildlife Division,
Species Conservation Branch,
Room 902C, Tollgate House,
Houlton Street, Bristol BS2 9DJ;
Telephone: 0117 9876154;
Fax: 0117 9878182.

Choose flowers at their peak.

picking them as each day of sunlight will gradually fade and age the bloom, which will result in a less colourful flower when pressed. It is best not to strip a plant of all its flowers in one go; take just a few so that the remainder can be enjoyed in the garden, by both you and the bees! Pick the flowers carefully and collect them in a basket, being careful not to crush any petals, then place them in the press as quickly as possible. Alternatively, if you are a little way from home, you can place the collected flowers in a polythene bag, being careful not to overcrowd them, then fill the bag with air and seal. The pocket of air will keep the flowers safe from damage and sealing the bag will prevent the flowers wilting until they can be pressed.

Always inspect flowers carefully before you pick them. The blooms should be in perfect condition as any damage or dirt will show up more once they are pressed. The same applies when choosing flowers from a florist. A good florist will be happy to tell you which day of the week their flowers are delivered, which will enable you to be sure of their freshness. Always choose bright, fresh-looking blooms, before they have started to produce any pollen, and those that show no sign of wilting or age. It is best not to be tempted by the older bargains; if a flower looks a little worn in the shop it will show in the final pressed result.

GATHERING MATERIAL FOR PRESSING

The most important point to remember when gathering plant material is that it should always be dry. Try to collect on a warm, sunny day to ensure that the flowerhead is both totally dry and fully opened to the sun. The time of day is also important; the optimum picking time is midday, when the morning dew has evaporated and before the damp of the evening settles in. Any dampness on a flower when pressed will cause mildew to form and the bloom will be no use. The mildew may also damage other material in the flower press.

It is important to press gathered material as quickly as possible. If flowers are left out of the press for any length of time they will start to shrivel and wilt and therefore be unsuitable for pressing.
If the sun is not shining and collecting can only be done on a damp day, pick the flowers with a stem attached, place them in a vase of water and bring them inside for a few hours. This will allow them to stay fresh while drying out; when fully dry, the flowers are ready to be pressed. Collected material should be handled as little as possible to prevent any bruising of the petals; if possible, hold the flower delicately by the stem.

KEEPING A DIARY OF SOURCES

It can be very helpful to keep a diary throughout the year as a record of flowers collected and pressed. On each day, enter the name of the flowers and foliage that have been pressed to give you some idea when the material will be ready for use in designs. It will also help to identify the pressed material when the flower press is first opened.

As well as entering the name of flowers, it is also a good idea to keep details in the diary of where the material was collected, particularly if picked from the wild. This information can prove invaluable in the following year, when you have forgotten the date and location they were found.

When collecting wild flowers, pick only a few of any one species.

Tools

A big advantage of the craft of flower pressing is that it does not need to be very expensive.
Apart from a basic flower press, there are several tools
that will be required for creative design work, but none of these should cost too much.

The following list of tools are all essential contents of a flower presser's toolbox:

🍃 **Large scissors** Used for cutting paper, fabric and bulky plant material.

🍃 **Small nail scissors** Invaluable for delicate work, such as removing a calyx, petals or thinning sprays.

🍃 **2B pencil** A soft pencil is ideal for designing picture layouts.

🍃 **Blunt-edged tweezers** Essential for gentle handling of all pressed flowers.

🍃 **Paintbrushes** Used for applying colour washes and stencilling; a good selection of sizes is ideal.

🍃 **Eraser** Preferably a soft white eraser, for removal of pencil lines.

🍃 **Craft sticks** These wooden sticks are used to apply small quantities of glue to pressed material. They can be purchased in art and craft shops or substituted with cocktail sticks.

🍃 **Scalpel** Use a scalpel with changeable blades for cutting delicate plant material.

🍃 **Ruler** A clear plastic one is best.

🍃 **Set square** This is useful when drawing picture layouts.

🍃 **Craft knife** Use this for cutting mounts, cards and papers.

The basic tool kit required for flower pressing.

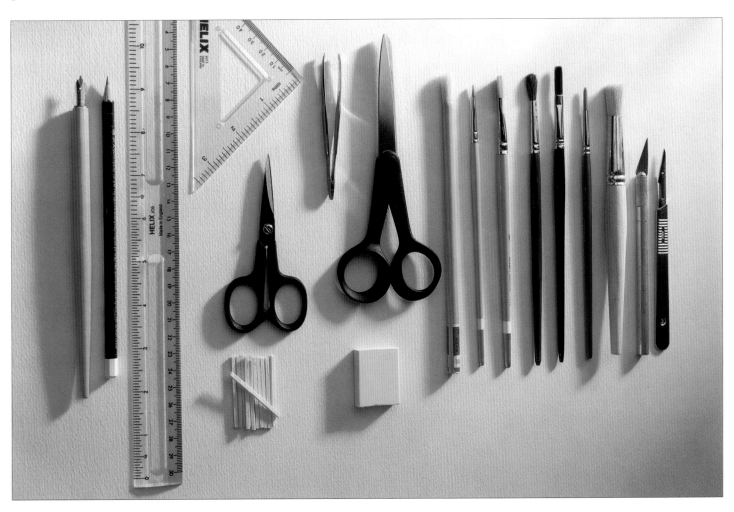

ART SUPPLIES

Many art products can be used to enhance your pressed flower work. Paint washes, stencilling and calligraphy can all add an extra dimension to pictures, and there is a vast selection of wonderful materials you can choose from.

The following list of materials are all used for the different projects featured in this book:

❦ **Watercolour paint** Ideal for border washes; a good selection of colours is required for creating tones to complement the pressed flower material.

❦ **Acrylic paint** Used to paint items such as the hat box (see page 64) and the papier mâché bowl (see page 72).

❦ **Glue** Select a general-purpose craft or paper glue that dries clear.

❦ Gold and silver paint Useful for seasonal decorations and cards; lovely when applied to skeletonized leaves.

❦ **Gold and silver pens** Used for seasonal highlighting and text.

❦ **Calligraphy pen and ink** Used for adding text to pressed flower pictures; requires some practice to master the technique.

❦ **Varnish** It is important to use a water-based, clear matt varnish. When applied, this can appear a milky white colour, but it clears when fully dry.

❦ **Stencils** Use either ready-cut stencils or create your own designs using a sheet of stencil card.

Paints, glues and stencil card will all be useful when creating pressed flower designs.

PAPER AND FABRIC

Paper and fabric are both very important additions to pressed flower designs as they add texture and depth of colour to pictures.

PAPER

There is a huge choice of suitable papers for pressed flower work, ranging from watercolour papers to handmade and Japanese fibre papers. Experiment with as many unusual papers as you can. They can often be the inspiration for a design and are readily available from art and craft shops. They can be incorporated into any design work, and rewarding results can easily be achieved.

Handmade papers are usually a little more expensive to buy, but worth the extra cost as their quality and texture can transform a flower picture. These papers are all individual in texture and weight; some are even embedded with fragments of onion skins, rice, leaves, bracken and flowers. Do not cut these papers with scissors since harsh edges do not suit their textures. Instead, leave natural torn edges to create a softer effect. Handmade papers are available in many colours, but most are natural shades which particularly complement herbal and autumn designs.

Watercolour paper should be used as the backing to designs where paint washes need to be applied. They are available in a choice of colours and weights. As a general rule, the larger the picture design, the heavier the weight of watercolour paper required.

Papers are also used in the process of flower pressing as absorbing layers within the flower press. Blotting paper is highly absorbent and can be reused many times. After using it in a press always dry it off thoroughly before using it again. This paper can be purchased in art shops but if you cannot find any, absorbent tissue or one-way nappy liners are good alternatives.

FABRIC

Fabric can be used to provide interesting backgrounds for pressed flower designs and there is a vast selection to choose from. Pressed flowers are best complemented by natural fabrics. Irish linen, calico and muslin all make neutral backgrounds and their natural colouring looks attractive when used with coarse hessian. There

Natural fabrics in soft colours will complement many pressed flower designs.

are many hessians to choose from and their rough texture works well in garden-themed pictures. Patterned cotton prints, especially checks, can continue the colour theme of a picture, but avoid any busy fabrics that will compete with the pressed flowers.

Dupion silks make lovely backgrounds for soft, feminine pictures. The addition of delicate lace trims can also complement bridal and baby pictures, but this is best kept as a subtle decoration. Avoid fabrics with a shiny surface which can detract from the plant material and looks unnatural. It can also be difficult to glue plant material to this sort of fabric.

Incorporating fabrics into pressed flower designs does not have to be expensive; small samples can look good if used with corresponding textured papers.

FRAMING

After creating a pressed flower design that you are pleased with, it is important to finish the design with a complementary picture frame. This will both protect your work from damage and dust and enhance the entire picture. Framing can be expensive, but there are several options to choose from, according to the size of your budget.

PROFESSIONAL FRAMING

This can be quite expensive, but you may consider it worth doing for a special design. Picture frames vary enormously, from traditional wooden, gilded, metal or paint-washed, to plain frames. A good framer should offer you a large selection to choose from. If you are unsure they should also be willing to offer you advice.

When deciding on a frame, try to imagine several points, such as where you wish to display the picture and what type of effect you wish to create. Does it need to fit in with other frames in the room? Do you wish for a modern, antique, dominant or discreet effect? Framing is very much down to personal taste

and how much money you wish to spend on the design. Take your finished work along to the framer and place selected frames around it. Then stand back from the picture, and view it from a distance. Does the picture stand out from the frame, or is the frame dominating the picture design?

You will also need to consider whether to use a mountboard around the picture. This can be cut into a circle, an oval, a rectangle, a square, or any other shape you choose, and can add depth to the finished picture. I always like to use a 5cm (2in) cut mount around my designs.

Mountboard is available in a wide selection of colours and in a choice of textures and different paint effects, such as marbled. Again, this is very much a personal choice, but as a general rule mountboards should complement both the colours of the design and the colour of the picture frame, without dominating the picture. Ask to have non-reflective glass fitted to the picture frame, which will allow the picture to be viewed clearly from any angle.

Paint-washed frame

Plain wooden frame

Traditional gilded frame

Antiqued wooden frame

OLD FRAMES

Many types of picture frame can be found by hunting in antique shops and bric-à-brac markets. There may be some damage to the frames, but with a little work they can be transformed, perhaps by stripping back the varnish to reveal the wooden frame below, or by experimenting with different paint effects. This can greatly reduce the cost of framing and can achieve attractive and individual results.

DO-IT-YOURSELF FRAMES

A great assortment of ready-made frame kits are widely available to purchase and these contain full instructions on their making up. Alternatively, you may wish to try making your own frames, but this will require some skill and practice, and you may need to consult specialist books.

SUCCESSFUL PRESSING TECHNIQUES

Flower pressing, like many crafts, does not offer a guarantee of success, but practice will often produce good results. However, there are some techniques that can improve the chances of success and these are covered below.

TRADITIONAL PRESSING TECHNIQUES

Almost everyone tries to preserve a few sentimental flowers at some time in their life, either from a wedding or perhaps a baby's birth, as these flowers are always of particular sentimental value. Invariably, however, the pressed results can be a disappointment, with brown faded blooms that are brittle and shatter when touched. Unfortunately, the craft of flower pressing does not offer a guarantee of success; it is more a case of experimenting with the various pressing methods and the different varieties of flower until a good result is achieved. However, there are some flower pressing techniques that can improve the chances of success, and these are covered in detail on the following pages.

The process of pressing flowers is to remove all the plant's natural moisture content, and it is vital that this is achieved as quickly as possible. By doing this, plant material will not decay in the flower press, but will dry and retain its natural fresh colours. There is, of course, a dramatic difference in the appearance of a fresh flower to one that has been pressed. After pressing, a flower takes on a flat form, which usually makes the flower larger in size and can also change its shape. This is dependent on how the flower was placed in the flower press, for example, front facing or in profile.

The colour of the flower also changes; even in the most successful pressing colour tones can vary. The most difficult colour to press with good results is white, as this colour invariably turns transparent or brown, but by experimenting with different methods disappointments can be kept to a minimum. Deep purple and red-toned flowers achieve a slightly darker, sometimes blackened, colour when pressed, while blue flowers usually retain their colours extremely well, sometimes developing a slightly darker and more intense hue than when fresh. Delphinium, borage and lobelia are a few examples of flowers that retain their lovely rich blues when pressed. Most yellow and orange flowers, such as narcissi and cowslip, produce a slightly darker, richer colour.

The endless variations of colour offered to the flower presser by foliage are important for many designs. These can vary from rusty reds to greens and black and it is therefore impossible to predict the final colour tone that can be achieved after pressing. Young fresh leaves tend to darken from green to brown in the press. An example of this is holly, which is best pressed when the leaves are very young and soft.

By experimenting with different pressing methods, it is always a surprise when the press is opened for the first time. If you learn from failures, good results and satisfaction will eventually be achieved.

Always allow plenty of space when arranging flowers in the press.

PREPARING PLANT MATERIAL

All plant material that is picked and collected for pressing should be handled gently. Use tweezers to hold small flowers and stems to prevent unnecessary bruising. When possible, remove flower stems and leaves before pressing. Flower stems contain a high quantity of moisture and should be pressed separately. Cut the stem just below the calyx, the thick green growth at the base of the flower, with sharp scissors.

Single blooms
These are much easier to press successfully than double varieties. The more layers of petals on a flower, the slower is the process of drying in the press. Single flowers should be placed in the press face down, with the calyx and stems removed and pressed separately.

Double blooms
To prevent decay and mildew forming when the flower is in the press, remove a few petals from double flowers with tweezers, to thin out the bloom. Multi-petalled flowers should be taken apart and the petals pressed

All plant material requires some preparation before it can be placed in the press.

individually. These can then be rebuilt into the original flower shape once the separate elements are pressed.

Spray flowers
Spray flowers can also require thinning to prevent flowers and stems being pressed on top of each other. This will stop marks being formed where the plant material overlaps. Any flowers that are removed for thinning should not be wasted, but pressed separately for another time. Some sprays of flowers, such as lobelia, gypsophila and forget-me-not, press well with their stems still in place.

Trumpet-shaped flowers
Trumpet-shaped flowers, such as daffodils, should be sliced in half and placed in the press in profile. Small flowers, such as narcissi, can be pressed face down.

Bulky material
Bulky plant material, such as rosebuds, should be sliced in two before pressing. Use a sharp knife or scalpel, first cutting through the calyx and then up through the petals lengthways. This will create two identical flowers for pressing. Place these sliced flowers cut-side down in the press (use the flat side for gluing the flower to the paper later). The same process applies for more unusual material such as vegetables and fungi.

A wide variety of vegetables, such as carrot, spring onion, beetroot and chilli, can be pressed with good results. These should all be cut lengthways in the same way as the rosebuds. When pressing vegetables, it is best to pick them young and very small, ideally the thinnings from the vegetable patch. Mature vegetables can also be pressed by cutting them into slices before placing them in the press. Mushrooms and toadstools can also be cut lengthways, or if small they can be pressed whole. Do not press any fungi that you cannot first identify as non-poisonous.

Multi-floret plants
These can be divided into individual flowers and pressed separately or, if they are small, the entire floret can be pressed as one. Be sure to press the stems as well, so that the complete plant can be reconstructed when pressed.

Unusual materials
Moss, bark and seaweed can all introduce different and interesting textures to your work. When preparing moss, make sure that any mud has been removed first. Seaweed should be gently washed in fresh water to remove any salt particles and then carefully dried with a cloth before pressing. Do not let seaweed dry out completely before pressing as it will become brittle and shatter. Try experimenting with other attractive and unusual plant material, such as blackberries, catkins and seedheads. The results might surprise you and will often be worth it.

<u>FLOWER PRESSES</u>

When first starting to press flowers as a hobby, there are several different choices of press available. It is not always necessary to purchase a flower press; a homemade press can prove to be an effective and inexpensive starting point.

If after some encouraging results with the basic press, the craft has caught your imagination, it may be worth investing in a screw thread press or making one yourself.

When collecting plant material from the countryside a portable, travelling press is ideal. This press consists of the same materials as the basic press but it is smaller in size for ease of carrying. Several thick, strong elastic bands are used to hold the press together, instead of the house bricks. The contents of this press can be

MAKING A BASIC PRESS
You will need:
- Two squares of plywood
- Squares of corrugated cardboard (the same size as the plywood)
- Newspaper
- Blotting paper
- 3 house bricks or 2 luggage straps

1. Place one plywood square down flat. This is the outer cover of the press.
2. Layer on the plywood a square of corrugated cardboard, several sheets of newspaper, and a sheet of blotting paper.
3. Place the fresh flowers on the blotting paper. Cover these with another piece of blotting paper, and several sheets of newspaper.
4. Build up this sandwich effect in layers if desired, to a maximum of six layers.
5. Place the second plywood square on top of the layers. Weigh down the press with three house bricks, or use two strong luggage straps to hold the press tightly together.

transferred to a stronger press when you return home. If no flower press is available, use a large, heavy book instead. Place the plant material between several layers of absorbent paper, making sure the book is well protected from any moisture damage, and apply pressure on top of the book with a weight.

Suitable absorbent material
To press plant material successfully it is very important to use highly absorbent layers in the press. These act as a sponge, removing the natural moisture of the plant, to avoid any rot forming. The best material to use is blotting paper, which can be dried out after use and then used again. One-way nappy liners and tissue paper are also very effective absorbent layers. Newspaper should not be placed directly against the plant material as the ink can transfer on to the petals. It is, however, a useful thick padding layer within the press.

<u>SECRETS OF SUCCESS</u>

When all your plant material has been carefully selected for pressing, there are a few guidelines to follow in order to achieve the best results from the flower press.

MAKING A TRAVELLING PRESS
You will need:
- Two small pieces of plywood
- Small sheets of corrugated cardboard (the same size as the plywood)
- Blotting paper
- Two strong elastic bands

1. Build up the layers in the same way as for the basic press.
2. Hold the two outer layers of the press together with two strong elastic bands.

1. Fill each layer of the press with plant material of a similar thickness so that the entire layer will receive an even pressure once the press is closed. If a layer consists of various thicknesses of plant material, the thicker items will prevent the flatter flowers from being pressed effectively and will give disappointing results.
2. Remove any hard seedcases or calyxes before pressing plant material. It is possible to press these pieces of the flower, but keep them on a separate layer of the press and reconstruct the flower when finished.
3. Leave plenty of space between plant material in the press. Once pressure is applied to the press the flowers will flatten and become larger in size. Overlapping material will leave obvious marks on petals and leaves when pressed and if any mildew is formed, this will quickly spread to touching flowers and leaves.
4. Carefully inspect all plant material for small insects before pressing; a trapped insect could eat its way

MAKING A SCREW THREAD PRESS
You will need:
- Four wing nuts and washers
- Squares of corrugated cardboard (the same size as the plywood)
- Newspaper
- Blotting paper
- Two squares of plywood
- Four threaded bolts

1. Build up the layers of the press in the same way as the basic press.
2. Attach threaded bolts and wing nuts to all four corners of the plywood outer covers. Tighten these bolts equally to apply even pressure to the contents.

through the plant material in the press.
5. When pressing succulent plant material such as fruit, fungi or vegetables, change the layers of absorbent paper in the press frequently, replacing with dry absorbent paper. Do not remove the plant material from the press when changing layers, as it will be very soft and fragile. Carry out this process daily for the first few days and thereafter weekly, until the succulent contents are fully dry.
6. Attach a label to the corner of each layer in this press and on this write the name of the plant and when it was pressed. This is invaluable when searching for particular flowers and also helps you to know when the plant material is ready for use.

When is pressing complete?
When the flower press is stored in an average household temperature, pressing is usually complete after six to eight weeks. This time can be greatly reduced with quicker drying methods. Plant material is completely pressed when it feels dry and crisp to the touch; if it feels cold and soft then pressing is not yet complete and the plant material should be returned to the press and checked again in a few days' time.

FASTER PRESSING TECHNIQUES

It is not always possible or convenient to wait from six to eight weeks for plant material to be fully pressed and ready to use in your designs. There can be times when quicker results are needed, perhaps for a special gift-wrapping or present. Thankfully there are ways to overcome this problem; but remember that most of these speedier pressing methods require a greater amount of attention to achieve satisfactory results.

Heat method
1. Place the filled flower press in a warm position, such as an airing cupboard or on a shelf above a warm radiator. Ensure that there is a good circulation of air around the press to prevent mildew forming. The press will only need a gentle heat and should never become hot; if it does, the plant content will literally cook!
2. Change the absorbent tissue or paper layers in the flower press frequently. Remove them carefully and replace with fresh layers of absorbent material every day for the first two or three days. This process can then be reduced to every second or third day until the plant contents are completely pressed and dry. This pressing technique reduces pressing time of plant material to two to three weeks.

The colour and shape of fresh flowers can change considerably as a result of pressing.

Ironing method

This pressing method is for emergencies and should only be carried out on very dry plant material, such as leaves, ferns, bracken and grasses. Don't try this on any succulent material as you will make a terrible mess!

1. To iron leaves, set the iron on its lowest temperature and gently iron the leaves flat.
2. Place the pressed leaves in a traditional flower press to keep them flat.
3. Before ironing ferns, bracken and grass heads, insert a protective layer of paper between the iron and the plant material.

Microwave method

A microwave oven can be used to press fresh plant material very quickly and effectively. It is also an essential method of pressing flowers such as stephanotis or orchids with any degree of success. First you need to make a sandwich board press.

MAKING A SANDWICH PRESS

You will need:
- Two small pieces of plywood
- Layers of absorbent tissue or paper
- Heavy glass weight

1. Cut the two pieces of plywood to fit on to the microwave turntable. These will be the outer covers for the press.
2. Place a layer of absorbent paper on top of one piece of plywood. Then place the fresh flowers on top.
3. Place the second piece of plywood on top of the flowers, then put the sandwich press in the microwave.
4. Place a heavy glass weight on the top of the press. Pottery weights should be avoided as these will interrupt the flow of microwaves in the oven and prevent the flowers from drying out evenly.

An example of a flower that has been pressed using the microwave method.

1. Place the flowers in the sandwich press, making sure that the flower faces are turned upwards.
2. Build the layers of the sandwich press and microwave the flowers for two minutes on three-quarter power.
3. Allow the flowers to cool down completely in the press for at least 15 minutes. Only when the plant material is completely cold can you assess how much more pressing time will be required in the microwave. If this process is hurried, it can quickly result in blistered flowers caused by overheating.
4. When the flowers are completely cold, check to see if they are still limp and soft; if so they are not completely dried, so repeat the microwaving process for another 30 seconds on three-quarter power. Leave to cool completely and then repeat in 30-second sessions, until the plant material is completely dry.
5. After microwaving, store all flowers in a basic flower press for a few weeks to ensure that they are completely finished.

Do not overload the sandwich press with plant material. Limit it to three or four flowers at a time, and do not place several layers of material in the press at the same time. This would increase the cooking time required to press the flowers and could damage the plant material.

Microwave pressing is best suited to strong, sturdy flowers rather than delicate ones, which can easily become fused to the plywood during the pressing process. This problem can be overcome by placing the delicate flowers in the press for only one minute on three-quarter power and then finishing the flowers off in a basic press.

There are a few disadvantages to using the microwave method. First, it is very time-consuming. Second, most flowers will reduce in size through this heat process. Third, it is also easy to over-heat plant material and cause brittleness and blistering to the flowers. However, this method of pressing can achieve some wonderful results and is worth experimenting with.

Flowers suitable for microwaving

Plant material suitable for this type of pressing can be found in the colour charts (pages 88-93). The following flowers can be pressed particularly successfully using the microwave method.

Stephanotis Remove the flower's calyx and then carefully cut off the flower's shank, to leave just the flower face. Place three or four flowers in the sandwich press and microwave for one minute on three-quarter power. Leave to cool, then remove the flowers to a basic press for a few weeks.

Single daisy chrysanthemum Lay several layers of soft tissue or nappy liner on to the base plywood board of the sandwich press. Place one single chrysanthemum flower face upwards on top of this. Place another layer of soft tissue on top of the flower and then lay the plywood on top. Chrysanthemums bruise very easily and require extra padding for protection. Microwave the flower for one minute on three-quarter power, then quickly remove the top layer of absorbent tissue from the flower face and replace just the press board. Leave to cool thoroughly. If more pressing time is required, press in 30-second sessions, cooling in between. When completely pressed, place the daisy chrysanthemum in a traditional press for a few days.

Cymbidium orchid Remove the centre tongue of the orchid with a sharp knife. This can be pressed separately. Lay the orchid face up in the sandwich press and microwave for one minute on three-quarter power. Leave to cool down for 15 minutes, then check to see if it is dry and stiff. If not, return the press to the oven for 30-second intervals, allowing to cool down in between. Orchids should be fully dried in the microwave; if not, discoloration can occur afterwards. Keep a close watch on these flowers - they can easily blister and become brittle - but if successfully pressed they retain their colours well.

Tulip Remove the tulip petals and lay these in the sandwich press. Microwave for two minutes on three-quarter power. Leave to cool, then transfer the petals to a traditional press for a few days. The tulip shape can then be reconstructed for use in pressed flower designs.

Specialist techniques

Part of the fun of pressing plant material is never knowing for sure what surprise results you can achieve. There may be a few failures, but by learning and experimenting with different methods many exciting and unusual materials can give rewarding results.

The following list of flowers, fruit and leaves gives specialist techniques that can help when pressing unusual plant material. If you fail, have another go!

Skeletonized leaves
Collect a varied assortment of summer leaves and leave them to soak in a bucket of rainwater for a few weeks. This will soften the leaves and, once rinsed, enable you to lightly brush away the outer leaf tissue, leaving the skeleton intact. Place these skeletons into a traditional press for a few days before using them in designs.

Bridal flowers
Pressing bridal flowers can be a difficult process as the flowers can be a little tired and worn by the end of the wedding day. It is very important that you receive the bouquet as soon as possible after the wedding, before the flowers wilt. Dismantle the bouquet carefully to avoid bruising the flowers. If the bouquet is wired, carefully remove all the wires. Place the fresh flowers into a plastic bag and put this into a fridge for a couple

A wide variety of fruit can be pressed successfully.

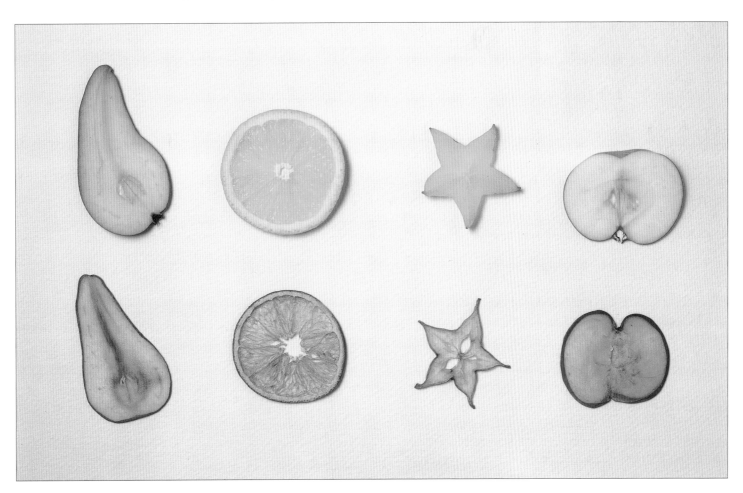

of hours; this can help to revitalize tired flowers a little. Use pressing methods suitable for the floral content of the bouquet, making sure you include plenty of foliage as well as the flowers.

Fruit and vegetables

A surprising selection of fruit can be pressed with good results. Always select fresh fruit and vegetables. Most fruit has a high water content and is best suited to microwave pressing techniques. Large fruit such as apples, pears, pineapples, kiwi fruit and oranges should be sliced thinly and pressed in a sandwich press in the microwave. They can then be finished off in a traditional press. Small succulent fruit such as strawberries and grapes should first be cut in half and then the soft centre of the fruit should be scooped out. The centres should then be gently filled with soft tissue paper and placed in a traditional flower press. This method can also be used on rose hips and berries.

Vegetables offer wonderful textures and interest to pressed designs, and they can also create many different shapes according to how they are prepared before pressing. Slice bulky vegetables in half lengthways and try to include some foliage as well in the press. They can also be cut thinly into cross-sectional slices for very different effects. Being easier to handle, fruit and vegetables are great fun for children to try pressing, even if they won't eat them!

Dried flowers

It is possible to press flowers that have previously been dried, although better results are always achieved with fresh blooms. To soften a spray of dried flowers hold them in the steam of a boiling kettle for a few minutes, but be careful not to scald your hands. These flowers can then be cut off the spray and pressed.

STORING PRESSED FLOWERS

Pressed flowers are very fragile and need protection from dust and direct sunlight. The best method of storing pressed flowers is to place them in small cellophane envelopes. These should not be overcrowded or the contents will be damaged; limit each envelope to 20 flowers. It is a good idea to use a cellophane envelope for one type and colour of flower as this can save a lot of time when you are trying to select flowers for a project. Store these envelopes in a set of small drawers or a filing cabinet for maximum protection from sunlight and dust.

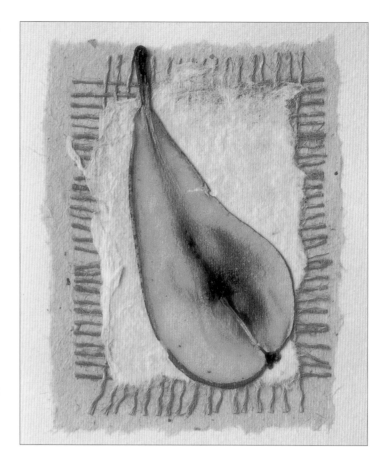

A detail from a pressed fruit greetings card.

DESIGNING WITH PRESSED FLOWERS

As mixing pressed flower colours can be a little daunting at first, the colour wheel can act as a helpful reference when blending colour tones together in a design.

USING COLOUR

The colour wheel comprises three primary colours - red, yellow and blue. A combination of two primary colours will create a secondary colour, for example yellow added to red will make orange. There are three secondary colours - orange, green and violet. Generally, it is best to use only two primary colours, for example red and yellow, together with the secondary colour orange created by mixing these two, in a design.

The use of colour is a very important element in creating flower pictures. Vibrant colours, such as red and orange, would suit a bold, modern design, while pastel shades are much more suited to soft, natural displays. Gaining confidence with colour will evolve gradually, but a good starting point is to decide whether you wish to create colour combinations that complement or contrast. Contrasting colours are found opposite each other on the colour wheel, for example orange and blue. By using the warmth of orange with

The colour wheel shows contrasting colours opposite each other. Colours next to each other create a more harmonious effect.

Here are a few examples of flowers from each section of the colour wheel:

Red: bougainvillea, geranium, lupin, poppy and rose
Orange: crocosmia, lily, nasturtium and wallflower
Yellow: chrysanthemum, daffodil, forsythia, mimosa and tulip
Green: astrantia, fern, helebore, hydrangea and nicotiana
Blue: bluebell, cornflower, delphinium, iris and pansy
Purple: anemone, freesia, larkspur, muscari and primula

For more details, refer to the Plant Colour Charts on pages 88-95.

Bright springtime flowers create a feeling of freshness.

the cool tones of blue, contrast is created in your composition. To create a harmonious coloured design, select colours that are adjacent to one another on the colour wheel, for example violet and blue; this will create a soft-toned picture.

As pressed plant material is natural, green tones can be used throughout most designs, but make sure it does not dominate the flower's colour tones. Pastel shades always mix together well, blending into a soft colour effect, for example pink and mauve. The colour should, of course, be continued with the background material of the design, by using soft shades of paper and fabric. The same theory applies to strong colour combinations, which should be backed with bold, vibrant papers.

Creating colour combinations is always down to personal taste, but when designing a pressed flower design, think of where it might eventually be displayed and create a design that is harmonious with your interior decor. It is a good idea before starting your picture to gather together small samples of pressed flowers, fabrics, papers and paints to be used in the work. Mix these samples together to form a sample sheet and then stand back from it to decide if the overall colour theme works well. By doing this first,

disappointment can be avoided later. However, colour is a personal choice so go with your own instinct. It is, after all, your opinion that counts.

CREATING MOODS WITH COLOUR

An interesting effect that can be achieved by careful selection of colours is mood. A good example of instant impact of mood, created by colour combinations, can be found in seasonal designs.

Spring
When we think of spring our thoughts are of young shooting leaves and flowers. Freshness can be conveyed by clean, bright colours such as the yellows of narcissi and primroses, the greens of young moss and the blues of periwinkles and bluebells.

Summer
A summery mood can be conveyed by using a colourful combination of flowers. This season brings a blast of all of nature's brilliant colours, which can be used to full effect with pressed plant material. Vivid mixes of reds, pinks, yellows and greens can be grouped in abundance by using pressed larkspur, roses, poppies, anemones and cow parsley.

The vibrant colours of these flowers convey a summery mood.

Autumnal colours create a feeling of mellow warmth.

Autumn

The season of autumn's mood is warm and mellow and this can be effectively portrayed by warm oranges, browns, creams and rusts. Pressed plant material includes skeletonized leaves, seedheads, pressed berries, fruit and fungi.

Winter

To reflect the season of winter, cool, icy-toned pressed flowers should be used. Give depth to winter designs by incorporating dark and blackened plant material as a background for cool silver and white tones. Holly leaves, ivy seedheads, snowdrops and lichen moss are ideal for reproducing the stark, cold tones of winter.

By being creative with colour and choice of plant material for pressing you can evoke many moods and atmospheres, which can be continued through a design by using suitable backgrounds and paint washes. Another mood that can be created by careful design is romance. To convey this mood the pressed flowers need to be gentle to the eye. Soft pinks and blues are ideal, especially if softened further by the use of sprays of flowers such as gypsophila and cow parsley, which create a gentle lacy effect (see the wedding sampler on page 76).

With careful colouring it is also possible to create moods that evoke both femininity and masculinity.

Feminine moods are suggested with soft pastel shades, while a more masculine mood is created with strong dark colours, greens, browns and black, as with pressed herbs and autumn leaves. A good example of this is the autumn picture (see page 58).

By being creative with the colour and choice of plant material for pressing we can evoke many moods and atmospheres. These can be continued through a pressed design by using suitable backgrounds and paint washes throughout the work. It is important to try to convey mood in your pressed work as this creates work that is rich in atmosphere and individuality.

COMPOSITION

The composition of your pressed flowers is the overall shape and design that you choose to create in your own work. It is also how you choose to arrange the individual pressed material within the design. Traditional forms of pressed flower compositions are usually limited to the shape of crescents, circles and S-shaped curves, but there is tremendous scope for far more contemporary designing with pressed flowers.

The following compositions are all used throughout this book; you may like to invent your own individual

The icy colours and spiky textures suggest a wintry mood.

An example of a labelled botanical composition.

designs or perhaps combine two different forms of composition to create something new and original.

Botanical

This type of pressed flower composition is clear and uncomplicated. Multiple pressed plant specimens such as herbs or culinary collections can be spaced throughout the design, with each specimen clearly labelled for reference. This form of composition can also be limited to a single plant specimen; here the plant can be shown in all its component forms - petals, roots, seedheads, flower in profile, leaves, seed, entire plant, and finally the flower in full face. This can look very attractive and interesting. A botanical composition is stylish and uncluttered and can be adapted for any size of pressed flower design.

Natural

A natural composition should be loose, informal and free-flowing, allowing the pressed plant material to look as it actually does in nature. There should be nothing false or unnatural about the design.

This form of composition is ideal for emphasizing the natural curves, spikes and characteristic textures of

A simple and natural style of composition.

A well-balanced geometric composition of regular shapes.

plants. Try to imitate the lines of a growing plant, including the complete flower with foliage and stem. The plant content should look as if it could still grow within the design.

Geometric

A geometric composition is formal in style, with well-defined outlines. These definitions can be created by background paint washes or strong lines formed from pressed flower stems. Geometric compositions should be well balanced and consist of regular shapes, sizes and colours. Bold pressed plant material is well suited to this type of picture, but try to avoid soft feathery sprays of flowers as these will weaken the strong elements of the work.

Collage

This type of composition gives great scope for incorporating other textiles and textures into your pressed flower work and creates an informal and haphazardly arranged picture. A good example of this is the autumn picture (see page 58), where a wide

variety of plant materials are displayed on different colours and textures of paper, adding interest and variety to the design.

Tapestry

This is a dense, colourful style of composition, where plant material is used to cover the picture completely. Any type of plant material can be used for this type of design, but careful use of colour combinations are required. If it is made too complicated the picture can become a mess. An example of this type of composition is the decorated hat box (see page 64), which is crammed with rich and vibrant colours.

These are just a few of the compositions I enjoy creating with pressed plant material. Use them as a starting point to develop your own style. Study fabric, garden layouts, wallpaper designs and, most importantly, nature for a wealth of inspiration.

TEXTURE

Texture in pressed flower work is a very important element of composition; a picture lacking it can look flat and uninteresting to the eye. Natural plant material offers many wonderful and varied textures, from coarse

The collage composition uses a variety of textiles and materials.

and rough-textured barks and seaweeds to smooth and soft petals, and from fragile and delicate sprays of tiny blossoms to sharp and spiky plants and grasses. Examples of all these different and contrasting textures should be reflected in your pressed flower work to provide the maximum interest.

Coarse texture

Coarse-textured plants are wonderful for adding extra interest to designs. All sizes of pictures require some texture, but generally the larger the picture the bolder can be the use of texture. Coarse materials produce the best contrasting effect when laid over smooth backgrounds of plant material, such as petals, rather than left with no backing.

There are so many coarse textured plant materials to use, ranging from extremely coarse lichen moss and barks, to berries, hips, sprays of catkins, seaweeds and grasses, and they can all be used to make bold additions to designs. In addition, pressed vegetables, onions, carrots, beans and fungi as well as flower seedheads should also play an important part in your compositions.

Right: This dense, colourful style of composition is reminiscent of stitched tapestry.

Below: Coarse-textured plants add bold interest.

Right: Smooth textures are useful for creating backgrounds or for forming focal points in a design.

Smooth texture

Smooth-textured plant materials are very adaptable for design work and complement all plant textures. They are particularly useful for creating flat backgrounds or for forming strong focal points in your designs. There is a wealth of smooth-textured plant material, but most is created from flower petals and some leaves. Anemones, roses, primroses, buttercups and geraniums are just a few of the flowers that offer a smooth and velvety texture.

Delicate texture

This pressed plant material offers a softening effect to pressed designs, by smoothing harsh lines or bold colours that may be too dominant in the work. Delicate-textured plant material tends to be sprays of flowers and foliage that are generally neutral in tone. Cow parsley, gypsophila and lady's-mantle are ideal for balancing against coarse and spiky materials, but there are many others to choose from, including delicate fronds of fern, fennel, clematis, southernwood and

Below: Delicate-textured flowers soften harsh lines and bold colours.

many seaweeds, which can all add softness and femininity to pressed flower designs.

Spiky texture
Tall, spiky plant material is ideal for adding height to a design. Lengths of long plant material give elegance to compositions, but they need to be kept in proportion with other textures and shapes of flowers. Plantain, grasses, agrimony, monkshood and loosestrife are just some of the examples of the pressed plants that can add vertical interest to your pressed flower work.

These different textures should be balanced within your compositions. Experiment with as many variations of texture as you can find. I always develop a picture first on paper, without gluing anything in place. This enables me to rearrange any material that may be unbalanced or too bold. Only when I am happy with the design will I begin to glue the elements in place.

BACKGROUNDS

Picture backgrounds are an essential element of a design. They add to the atmosphere of your work and blend all the elements of the picture together, creating a wide variety in moods and textures.

Paint-washed backgrounds
Paint-washed backgrounds can give a wide range of colours and effects to compositions. Apply watercolour washes with a wide soft brush on to watercolour paper. Test the colourwash first on scrap paper and when dry, check that the paint tone is complementary to your plant material. Always mix enough paint with water to complete the entire wash in one go.

Before applying the wash, moisten the paintbrush with water and dampen the paper to help it achieve an even absorption of paint. Load the paintbrush with the paint and, starting from the top of the paper, work across with even strokes until the entire area is covered. You will probably need to reload the brush a few times. For neutral-coloured plant material, paint-washed back-grounds should be kept very subtle in colour, whereas more vibrant flowers can be backed by strong washes.

Paper backgrounds
Paper backgrounds can be kept simple with just one coloured paper or varied by layering different sizes, colours and textures of paper on top of each other. Allow glued background papers to dry before applying

Spiky material adds height and elegance to a design.

pressed flowers to them, otherwise the papers can buckle. Heavily textured papers suit bold plant material; avoid using these with smooth material.

Fabric backgrounds
Fabrics also make lovely backings for pressed designs and can be combined with textured papers for endless variations. Avoid intricately patterned fabrics, as these will compete with the flowers. Try out different colours and weights of fabric, but always ensure that the edges are well glued to the backing paper to avoid fraying.

All backgrounds can be altered by gluing wispy pressed foliage such as skeletonized leaves over the top. These leaves are ideal for softening bright colours.

PATCHWORK PICTURE

This pressed flower design is reminiscent of an old stitched quilt. The patchwork style can easily be achieved with only a small selection of pressed material, and incorporating fabric and hand-made papers can add extra texture and interest to the final patchwork effect. The finished work creates a traditional Victorian feel which would look attractive in a cottage-style bedroom.

YOU WILL NEED

Pencil

Ruler

Artist's watercolour paper

Watercolour paint

Water

Paintbrush

Eraser

Fabric samples

Handmade papers

Glue

Pressed flowers

Pressed flower stems

FLOWER KEY
A Daisy B Monkshood C Delphinium
D Forget-me-not E Senecio F Hogweed
G Lavender H Hyacinth

1 Using a pencil and ruler, draw the picture design on to watercolour paper (see line drawing). Mix up a paint wash using blue watercolour paint and water and, using a fine paintbrush, paint alternate diamond shapes, keeping carefully within the pencil lines. Then paint the border surround, mixing enough paint to apply the wash in one go. Any delay will cause hard lines to form. Leave to dry, then erase all pencil lines.

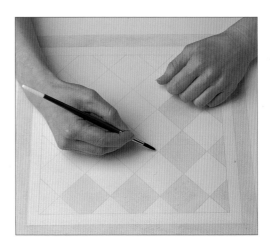

2 Choose and cut your selection of fabric and handmade paper pieces to fit within the diamond shapes. Place these pieces on to the design, rearranging them if necessary until you are happy with the overall balance of patterns. Then stick the pieces in their final position with glue. Repeat this process for the flowers and floral border.

3 Finally, arrange the pressed plant stems on the design to define the diamond shapes. Cut the stems to length, apply minimum glue to them and stick them into the final position. The completed design is now ready to be mounted and framed.

SPRING WOODEN TRUG

The arrival of spring is an exciting and welcome change from the cold winter months. There is a great variety of spring flowers and foliage suitable for pressing of which I have used a small selection. Primroses, snowdrops, cowslips and daisies are complemented with pussy willow, hazel catkins and ferns to cover all four sides of the wooden trug.

YOU WILL NEED

Paintbrush

Wooden trug

Emulsion paint

Stencil

Stencil brush

Paper towel

Pressed spring flowers and foliage

Glue

Water-based matt varnish

TIP
When stencilling a motif, ensure that the stencilling brush is almost dry. Too much paint on the brush might cause the stencil to smudge.

1 Using a medium-sized paintbrush, paint the entire wooden trug in light yellow emulsion paint. When completely covered, leave to dry for several hours and then apply a second coat of paint to achieve an even colour all over. Leave to dry overnight if possible.

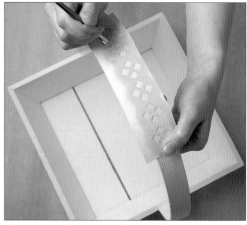

2 Using the stencil template on page 94 or another stencil of your choice, stencil over the trug handle. Using a deep yellow emulsion, apply the paint with a stencil brush. Dip the brush into the paint, dab the brush on a paper towel to work the paint out of the brush until it is almost dry, then dab the brush through the stencil.

3 Arrange the pressed spring material on to each side of the trug to make a pleasing design. When you are satisfied with the colour balance, glue the elements into place. Leave to dry.

4 Brush water-based matt varnish evenly over the entire trug. Cover all the pressed material to prevent damage. The varnish may look milky at first, but will turn clear when dry.

BABY'S BIRTH SAMPLER

This pretty pastel baby sampler has been designed to celebrate the special occasion of a child's birth. In soft shades of blue and pink, it could be a suitable gift for either a boy or a girl. I wanted to use the language of flowers in this keepsake and so chose daisy, which means innocence, rose for love and gypsophila which is also known as baby's breath.

YOU WILL NEED

Soft pencil

Artist's watercolour paper

Watercolour paint

Paintbrush

Handmade papers

Glue

Scissors

Ruler

Calligraphy pen

Eraser

Lavender heads and stems

Pressed flowers

FLOWER KEY
A Forget-me-not **B** Geranium **C** Lady's mantle **D** Larkspur **E** Daisy **F** Hyacinth **G** Rose **H** Cow parsley **I** Senecio **J** Stock **K** Gypsophila **L** Marguerite **M** Lavender

1 Draw the picture layout on to watercolour paper (see line drawing). Paint the outside border, first painting the pink and, when dry, painting the blue, to avoid any colour runs. Select three different handmade papers. Tear one piece into a square to fit just inside the painted border; glue in place. Tear the second paper into a smaller square; glue it on top. Repeat with a third square. Cut a square of watercolour paper, and colourwash it in pale pink.

3 Space pressed larkspur evenly around the colourwashed centre and glue in place. Glue a floral border around the centre of the picture on to the larger square of handmade paper. Then glue small pressed flowers on to the lattice border. Finally, cut lavender stems to length and glue these over the pencil lines to divide the lattice-work border.

2 Glue the colourwashed square on to the centre of the picture and leave to dry. Mark two faint pencil lines on the square. Using these as guidelines, print neatly the name and date of birth of the baby with a calligraphy pen. Leave to dry, then erase the pencil lines. Glue single lavender heads around the square.

FLORAL CANDLE

In recent years candles have increased in popularity and many specialist candle shops have now opened. I have chosen to decorate a very large, plain church candle with bold vertical stripes of yellow and blue pressed flowers. The design is most effective when made with flowers of intense colours, and by varying the shape and size of the vertical stripes, more definition is created.

YOU WILL NEED

Ruler

Scalpel

Large plain church candle

Pressed flowers

Glue

Water-based matt varnish

Paintbrush

Glass dome (optional)

NOTE
This candle is meant for decorative purposes only. If you intend to light it, make sure the varnish is water-based and do not leave the candle unattended when lit.

1 Using a ruler and a scalpel, gently draw a vertical line from the top of the candle to the base. Make sure that this line is actually vertical and not veering slightly to the right or the left, as this will act as the starting point for gluing on all the vertical stripes of pressed flowers.

2 Select the pressed flowers to be used; try to use similar-sized flowers of each type. Starting with the blue delphiniums, glue these along the marked line on the candle. Space the flowers along the line so that whole flowers can be used at the candle base. Continue with the remaining vertical stripes around the candle, alternating the colours and stripes until the entire candle is covered.

3 When the pressed flowers have dried to the candle, apply a layer of water-based matt varnish over the entire candle. Apply this gently with a very soft brush using vertical strokes, ensuring that all the flowers are sealed. Leave to dry for several hours. The candle can now be displayed in the glass dome if desired.

HERB KNOT GARDEN

This intricate pressed herb picture is based on a knot garden design. Most herbs press successfully, particularly thyme, rosemary and fennel. Lavender stems are used to divide the garden borders, with paint-washed paths in between.

YOU WILL NEED

Pencil

Ruler

Artist's watercolour paper

Watercolour paint

Paintbrush

Eraser

Pressed herbs

Calligraphy pen

Lavender stems

Glue

Handmade papers

Hessian

FLOWER KEY
A Borage **B** Rosemary **C** Sage **D** Curry
plant **E** Fennel **F** Thyme **G** Lavender
H Rue **I** Sorrel **J** Southernwood
K Marjoram **L** Mint

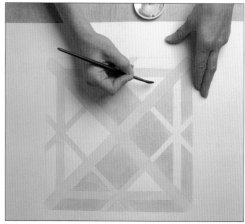

1 Draw the garden layout in pencil on watercolour paper (see line drawing). Mix the watercolour paint washes. Paint the centre and outer borders in a neutral brown and the garden paths in green. Keep carefully within the pencil lines, then leave to dry. Erase any visible pencil lines.

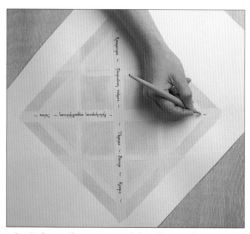

2 Select the pressed herbs to be used in the design. Using a calligraphy pen, write the herb names in Latin along the four main diagonal garden paths. It is a good idea to try this out first on a separate sheet of paper to ensure that the word spacing is equally balanced. Leave to dry.

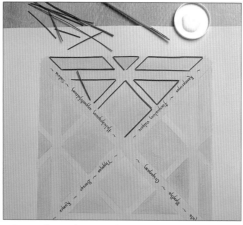

3 Define the garden design with lavender stems. Cut the stems to length, then stick them on the pencil lines around the garden borders. Work in stages. When one area is complete, place a weight on top until the glue has dried, then continue.

4 Tear small pieces of handmade paper to fit within the garden borders and stick them in place. Cut hessian to the size of the central four squares and glue it to the picture. Finally, arrange the pressed herbs on to the garden and glue in place.

SEASIDE PHOTO FRAME

The shoreline provides many exciting and unusual materials that are suitable for pressing. I love to go beachcombing for varying colours and shapes of seaweed, lichen moss, seedheads and weather-beaten barks for my pictures. Seaweed provides the backbone of this design, while sprays of pressed monkshood, lichen moss, fennel and hydrangea decorate the corners.

YOU WILL NEED

Photo frame

Emulsion paint

Paintbrush

Stencils of seahorse and shell

Stencil brush

Paper towel

Handmade paper

Glue

Scissors

Coarse string or twine

Shells

Star fruit

Pressed plant material

NOTE

After washing seaweed, dry it with a cloth and then press it when still supple. If left to dry, the seaweed will become brittle and break when pressed.

1 Remove the glass from the photo frame to avoid marking it with paint. Apply a coat of natural-coloured emulsion paint over the entire frame, and leave to dry. Then apply a second coat of the same colour of paint to achieve an even tone. Allow to dry.

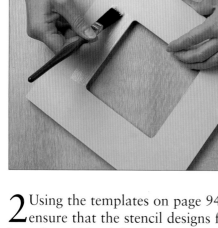

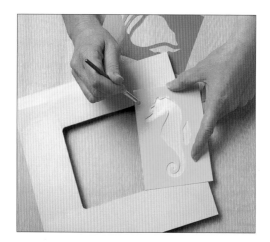

2 Using the templates on page 94, ensure that the stencil designs fit into the width of the frame. Dip a stencil brush in white emulsion paint and dab the brush through the stencils on to the frame. Stencil the seahorse motif on the vertical sides and the shell to the horizontal sides of the frame, ensuring that the motifs are centred on each side. Allow the paint to dry.

3 Tear three small squares of natural-toned handmade paper. Glue one paper square to a corner of the frame, centring the paper on the corner. Repeat with the two remaining paper squares to decorate two further corners of the frame, leaving the lower corner undecorated.

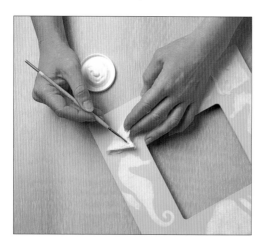

4 Cut four lengths of coarse string or twine to fit exactly the inner edges of the photo frame. Apply glue carefully to the back of the string with a fine paintbrush and stick the lengths to the frame, butting up the corners. Leave to dry.

5 Glue a few shells and star fruit slices to the lower corner of the frame. Arrange pressed plant material on the frame, without gluing it into place. Position larger items such as seaweed first, then arrange smaller flowers, moss and shells on top of this. Try to create flowing lines that do not end abruptly. When you are satisfied with the design, glue the pressed materials in place.

Seaweed, shells and slices of starfruit are combined to make a highly textured and three-dimensional frame, which would look very attractive displayed on a bathroom shelf with other seaside mementoes.

GREETINGS CARDS

It is always very special to receive a greetings card from someone who has taken the time and effort to make it by hand. These contemporary cards, which are interlined with plain paper on which to write a message, are all made from various pressed flowers and fruits, showing that a wide variety of effects can be achieved with very few materials.

YOU WILL NEED

Scissors

Artist's watercolour paper

Ruler

Handmade papers

Glue

Hessian

Pressed fruit and flowers

Raffia

String

Watercolour paint

Paintbrush

Fabric remnants

Fuse wire

IVY LEAF CARD

1 Cut a piece of cream watercolour paper into a rectangle measuring 14.5 x 10.5cm (5³/₄ x 4¹/₄in). Fold the paper in half widthways to form a card. Next cut a piece of cream hand-made paper to the same measurements. Glue this to the middle of the card. Leave to dry.

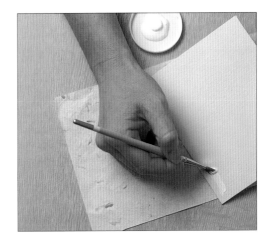

2 Choose two different natural-toned handmade papers and tear two rectangles from each paper to measure 5 x 3.5cm (2 x 1³/₈in). Glue these four pieces of paper to the card to form a quartered rectangle, centred on the card. Any rough edges should overlap the other quarter. Leave to dry.

3 Glue a yellow rose leaf to one quarter of the rectangle, then glue another rose leaf to the quarter diagonally opposite. Glue two green ivy leaves to the remaining rectangles. Finally, make a small bow out of a length of raffia and glue this to the centre of the card.

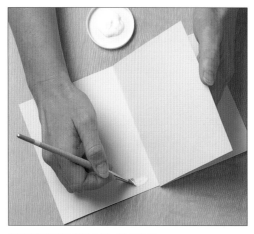

PRESSED PEAR CARD

1 Cut a piece of cream watercolour paper into a rectangle measuring 24 x 15cm (9^1/$_2$ x 6in). Fold this in half widthways to form the greetings card. Tear a piece of textured hand-made paper to measure 12 x 9.5cm (4^3/$_4$ x 3^3/$_4$in), and glue this to the centre of the card front.

2 Cut a rectangle of hessian, slightly smaller than the textured paper and then glue this to the centre of the card. Tear a small rectangle of a light-coloured handmade paper and glue it on to the hessian. Leave to dry. Finish the card by gluing a sliced pressed pear on the front.

Make the remaining three greeting cards using similar methods:

SQUARE HEART CARD

Make this from two layers of textured papers, torn into a heart shape and glued to the basic card. Glue a spray of pressed pink stocks and gypsophila on to the paper and finish the card with a natural string bow.

DELPHINIUM CARD

Layer the basic greetings card with a rectangle of handmade paper and then a smaller rectangle of watercolour paper. Apply a blue watercolour paint wash, then glue on two small squares of co-ordinating checked fabrics. Finally, glue a spray of gypsophila and a pressed delphinium to the centre of the card, and small larkspur flowers to the vertical sides of the paint-washed paper.

SILVER WIRE CARD

Layer the card with a textured white paper and overlay this with three small squares of different, natural-toned papers. Glue pressed senecio, lichen moss and a clematis seedhead on to the squares. Cut two pieces of raffia 4cm (1^1/$_2$in) long. Tie each piece of raffia around a 7cm (2^3/$_4$in) length of silver fuse wire. Bend the wires to form an 'S' shape, and glue them to the greetings card.

BOTANICAL PICTURE

This simple and striking botanical picture is quite easy to create, needing only one specimen of each species. Choose material in a variety of colours, as this will help to give an overall balance to the design, while different sizes, shapes and textures will add further interest.

YOU WILL NEED

Scalpel and cutting board

Mount

Artist's watercolour paper

Masking tape

Pencil

Ruler

Eraser

Calligraphy pen

Pressed flower material

Glue

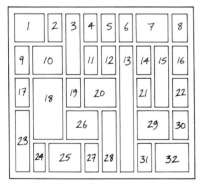

FLOWER KEY
1 Acer 2 Statice 3 Larkspur 4 Gypsophila
5 Fuchsia 6 Snapdragon 7 Clematis
8 Crocosmia 9 Lavender 10 Sweet pea
11 Broom 12 Snowdrop 13 Barley
14 Forget-me-not 15 Heather
16 Wallflower 17 Southernwood 18 Poppy
19 Lady's-bedstraw 20 Euphorbia
21 Holly 22 Tansy 23 Agrimony 24 Sorrel
25 Fennel 26 Laburnum 27 Rosemary
28 Chilli 29 Hogweed 30 Geranium
31 Willow 32 Delphinium

1 Using a sharp scalpel and a cutting board, carefully cut out the required shapes in the mount, to fit the pressed plant material. Attach a sheet of watercolour paper to the back of the mount with a piece of masking tape. The mount should be able to be lifted up to reveal the art paper beneath.

2 Using a pencil and ruler, draw two pencil lines at the base of each shape as guides for placing the Latin names. Then, using a calligraphy pen, neatly write the relevant plant names on to the watercolour paper. Spacing of the letters is important; practise first on a piece of scrap paper. When all the lettering is complete, allow to dry for several hours. Then erase any pencil marks.

3 Choose pressed flower specimens that will fit easily within the mount size and, using a minimum amount of glue, stick one flower into the centre of each cut-out opening. When the picture is complete, secure the watercolour paper to the back of the mount by taping around all the edges. The design can now be framed.

HERB BOTTLES

These bottles of oil and vinegar are simple to make and look very attractive when displayed on a kitchen shelf or windowsill. Any shape or design of bottle can be decorated with pressed herbs, spices and vegetables to reflect the contents of the bottle. Sealed with a cork stopper, these decorated bottles would make lovely gifts that can be refilled when empty.

YOU WILL NEED

Handmade papers

Glass bottle with cork

Glue

7.5cm (3in) square of stiff card

Pencil

Scissors

Hole punch

Coarse-textured string or raffia

Pressed herbs and vegetables

Funnel

Wine vinegar or oil

1 Tear a rough-edged square of handmade paper to fit on to the front of a glass bottle, then carefully glue it in position. Then tear a smaller square of contrasting-coloured handmade paper and glue this diagonally on top of the first piece of paper. Leave to dry.

2 To make a tag for the bottle, fold the square of stiff card in half and draw from the fold a diamond shape 4cm (1¹/₂in) wide, so that the fold forms one side of the diamond. Cut out the diamond shape, leaving the folded edge to form a card. Using the same paper as the label, cut a piece just large enough to cover the folded card on both sides, and glue to the card. Tear a smaller diamond shape in a darker paper and glue this to the front of the tag. Leave to dry.

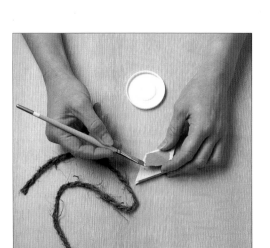

3 Using a paper punch, make a hole at the top of the back of the tag and thread through a piece of coarse-textured string or raffia. Tie the tag securely around the bottle neck. Select the pressed herbs and carefully glue them on to the label and tag. Using a funnel, fill the bottle with vinegar or oil and seal the bottle with a cork.

VEGETABLE LONG TOM POT

One of the most rewarding aspects of pressing can be experimenting with unusual plant material, such as vegetables. This terracotta long tom pot has been handpainted and decorated with a variety of pressed vegetables to produce a wonderfully colourful effect.

YOU WILL NEED

Paintbrushes

Emulsion paint

Terracotta long tom pot

Scissors

Hessian

Glue

Coarse garden string

Pressed vegetables

Matt varnish

TIP
Any bulky vegetables should be sliced in two lengthways before being pressed.

1 Using a paintbrush, apply a coat of cream emulsion paint to the upper lip and base of the pot. When dry, paint darker yellow freehand diamond shapes around the top. Leave to dry.

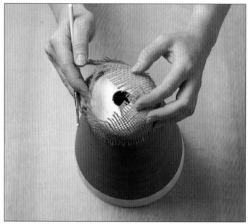

2 Cut the hessian to fit around the base of the pot. It should be 7cm (2³/₄in) in depth. Glue the hessian to the pot. Then glue coarse string around the edges of the hessian.

3 Select the pressed vegetables to be used. Using glue sparingly, stick the vegetables to the terracotta pot, grouping some vegetables together, until you have covered the entire pot. This should be done in slow stages to avoid damage as the pot is rotated.

4 When the vegetables are firmly stuck, apply a matt varnish to the entire pot. This is best applied with a soft brush, being careful not to lift any of the pressed material. Leave to dry overnight if possible. The pot is now ready to be filled.

FRUIT PICTURE

This contemporary fruit picture shows what attractive results can be achieved when pressing fresh fruits. The design contains pressed apple, orange, star fruit and pear, but many other fruits can be pressed successfully, including the more exotic ones, such as kiwi or pineapple slices. Always select very fresh, firm fruit, avoiding any that are over-ripe or bruised.

YOU WILL NEED

Artist's watercolour paper

Mount

Masking tape

Handmade papers

Glue

Four slices of pressed fruit

Frame

TIP
Fruit has a high water content, so to prevent any rot or decay forming, it is best to press it quickly using the microwave method (see pages 19 and 22).

1 Cut out a piece of watercolour paper to the same size as the mount. The mount should measure 36cm (14³/₈in) square with four individual squares measuring 8cm (3¹/₄in) cut out of the centre. Secure the watercolour paper to the back of the mount with masking tape.

2 Select various colours and textures of handmade paper and place them in the four square cut-outs; vary each square to add interest to the picture. When you are happy with your selection, glue them in place and then leave to dry.

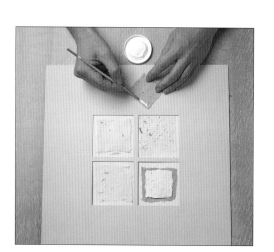

3 Finally, select the pressed fruit and place on to the handmade papers. When you have decided on the overall balance of the picture, stick the fruit in place using a minimum amount of glue. Leave to dry for several hours. The picture is now ready to frame.

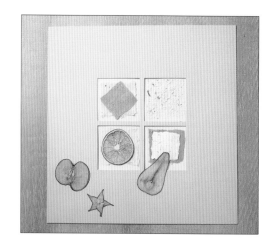

SHAKER BOX

These attractive storage boxes were first designed by a religious group called the Shakers who believed that items should be kept to a simple order and made with excellent craftsmanship. With this in mind, I have kept the pressed flower decorations to a minimum, with yellow-toned flowers arranged around the oval box and a simple border of foliage and flowers around the oval lid.

YOU WILL NEED

Pressed yellow flowers and foliage

Wooden Shaker box

Glue

Paintbrush

Water-based matt varnish

Plan your flower design on paper first before gluing the pressed flowers in position on the box.

1 Choose an assortment of delicate pressed flowers to decorate the Shaker box. Starting from the front of the box, carefully glue the flowers on to the sides. Use tweezers to place the fragile flowers to avoid damaging them. Try to vary both the height and shape of the flowers as you go around the sides of the box.

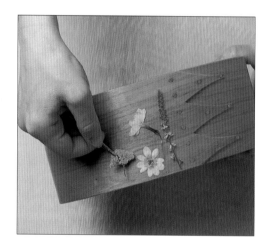

2 Arrange a row of overlapping rose leaves around the Shaker box lid and then glue in place. Arrange pressed celandines evenly on top of the rose leaves to form a ring, and glue in place. In the centre of the lid glue a spray of delicate narcissi and leave to dry.

3 Using a soft paintbrush, gently cover all the pressed plant material with clear matt varnish, ensuring that all the pressed plant material is completely sealed. The varnish will appear milky when first applied, but will dry clear. Leave the varnish to dry.

AUTUMN PICTURE

Autumn, my favourite season, offers a huge variety of mellow tones and textures suitable for pressing, ranging from rich yellow, bronze and red leaves to fungi, leaves, moss, bark, berries and seedheads. This pressed design uses blackberries, honesty and sycamore seedheads, mushrooms and green moss to represent the season's glorious colours.

YOU WILL NEED

Hessian

Scissors

Glue

Artist's watercolour paper

Handmade papers

Pressed plant material

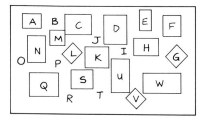

FLOWER KEY
A Sycamore B Ivy C Maple D Oak
E Euphorbia (*on paper*) F Walnut G
Blackberry H Honesty I Euphorbia
J Holly K Bark (*on paper*) L Mushroom
M Poppy seedhead N Rose
O Monkshood P Fern Q Berberis R Bark
S Clematis seedhead T Bryony U Tree of
heaven V Hawthorn W Moss

TIP
Slice any bulky material in half to reduce the depth of the picture.

1 Cut a piece of hessian measuring approximately 45 x 26cm (18 x 10³/₈in). Leave a frayed edge for a softer line. Apply glue sparingly to the hessian; excess glue will come through the fibres and show in the final picture. Stick it to the centre of the watercolour paper and leave to dry.

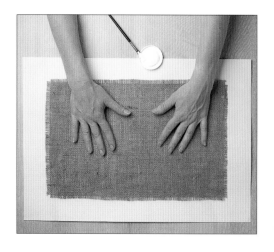

2 Tear assorted handmade papers into various shapes and sizes to suit the available pressed material. Arrange the paper pieces on the hessian to form a collage effect and then glue in place.

3 Arrange the pressed plant material on the picture. Rearrange the pieces to achieve a balance of texture and colour, then glue in position.

WOODEN TRAY

This decorated wooden tray features pressed foliage and flowers in natural green tones. The tray was first colourwashed in cream and green acrylic paints and then decorated with stencil borders. Pressed green ferns interwoven with hop vines were glued around the inner edge, then a border of small green ivy leaves completed the decoration.

YOU WILL NEED

Fine sandpaper

Wooden tray

Damp cloth

Emulsion paint

Paintbrushes

Acrylic paints

Diamond stencil

Stencil brush

Paper towel

Flower stencil

Pressed plant material

Glue

Water-based matt varnish

1 Lightly rub the surface of the tray with fine sandpaper, following the wood grain. This will roughen the surface, enabling the paint to adhere better. Wipe with a damp cloth to remove any dust; leave to dry. Apply a coat of white emulsion paint over the tray. When dry, apply a coat of cream acrylic paint and leave to dry.

2 Using a large brush, apply a thin wash of green acrylic paint to the inside base of the tray. Leave to dry. Next, using a small paintbrush, carefully paint the upper edge of the tray and inside edges of the handles with dark green paint. Leave the tray to dry thoroughly before continuing on to the next stage.

3 Stencil a diamond border around the outer edge of the tray base with dark green paint (see page 94). Leave to dry. Then stencil a flower border around the outside of the tray.

4 Glue ivy leaves on the base of the tray to form a border just inside the stencil design. Glue ferns and hops to the inner sides of the tray. When dry, apply two coats of matt varnish.

ANEMONE PICTURE

The wonderfully rich assortment of colours offered by anemones provided the inspiration for this bold, bright picture. Various shades and sizes of anemones were used to create the border, while in the centre were arranged a selection of pressed flowers in toning colours.

YOU WILL NEED

Artist's watercolour paper

Pencil

Ruler

Watercolour paints

Paintbrush

Eraser

Handmade paper

Glue

Lavender stems

Pressed flowers

1 Draw out the picture on to watercolour paper using a fine pencil. Apply an even wash to the wide outer border with cerise watercolour paint. Then apply a deeper mauve paint wash to the inner border, keeping within the pencil lines. When dry, gently erase the pencil border lines.

2 Select a bright, textured handmade paper for the central squares of the picture. Gently tear 16 squares of this to fit easily within the pencil lines already marked. Leave a rough and natural edge to the paper. Glue in place and leave to dry.

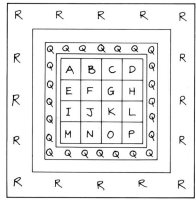

FLOWER KEY

A Anemone (small) **B** Stock
C Monkshood **D** Tree of heaven
E Delphinium **F** Fuchsia **G** Primrose
H Larkspur **I** Periwinkle **J** Poppy
K Pansy **L** Geranium (pink) **M** Lobelia
N Geranium (purple) **O** Geranium (red)
P Dianthus **Q** Purple larkspur
R Anemone

3 Place long, straight lavender stems, cut to length, on the pencil lines dividing the 16 central squares. Glue in position. Do this in stages, leaving each stage to dry before continuing. Arrange the pressed flowers into the squares, then glue them in place.

4 Arrange pressed purple larkspurs on the inner border until they are equally spaced around the central square; glue in place. Position pressed anemones around the outer border, alternating the colours. Glue in place. The picture can now be framed.

HAT BOX

The vibrant colours of purple geranium, delphinium, berberis and monkshood, with shades of pink sweet peas, larkspur and deep red field poppies have been chosen to decorate this hat box. The pressed flowers have been arranged to look like découpage, the art of decorating furniture and small items with cut-out scraps of paper and prints.

YOU WILL NEED

Hat box

Paintbrush

Acrylic paint

Pressed flowers

Glue

Water-based matt varnish

Co-ordinating ribbon

1 Paint the entire hat box, inside and out, with pink acrylic paint and leave to dry. This is best done in stages for ease of handling. Apply a second coat of paint and leave to dry. The paper box may absorb the paint unevenly; if so, a third coat may be needed to achieve an even tone.

2 Select a wide variety of pressed flowers to decorate the lid. Starting from the outside edge of the top surface, glue the pressed flowers to the lid, gradually working towards the centre. Overlap the flowers slightly to avoid leaving any gaps. Decorate the sides of the lid in the same way.

3 When dry, apply a coat of varnish over the box using a soft paintbrush Leave to dry thoroughly and then repeat with a second coat, until the flowers are completely sealed. Leave to dry overnight.

4 Make a large ribbon bow for the top of the hat box, and leave two long tails from the bow. Lay the ribbon on the box lid, take the two ribbon tails to the inside of the lid, and glue to secure.

WHITE MIRROR

This fresh, bright mirror features white and silver pressed plant materials, chosen for their colour, bold texture and shape, backed by assorted handmade papers, sheet music and silver paint. Created from a rough wooden frame, the surround was first painted white, then lightly sanded to achieve a weather-beaten effect, before being decorated with pressed material.

YOU WILL NEED

Paintbrushes

Wooden mirror frame

Emulsion paint

Fine sandpaper

Damp cloth

Handmade papers

Silver paint

Sheet music

Glue

Pressed plant material

Water-based matt varnish

1 Using a large paintbrush, paint the entire frame with white emulsion, and leave to dry. Repeat with a second coat, and allow to dry again. Lightly rub over the painted surround with fine sandpaper, following the wood grain. This will remove small areas of paint and achieve a weather-beaten effect. Wipe over with a damp cloth to remove any dust and leave to dry.

2 Tear eight small strips of smooth-textured, white handmade paper the same width as the frame. Using metallic silver paint and a fine paint-brush, carefully paint several wavy lines on each strip of paper.

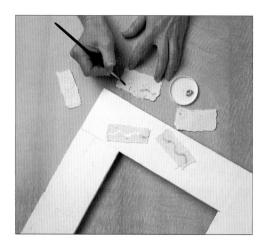

3 Tear pieces of textured handmade paper into various sized squares no wider than the mirror frame. Repeat with the sheet music. Space the textured and music paper pieces around the mirror frame, one on each corner and one in the centre of each side, varying the combinations, then glue into place. Then glue the paper strips that are decorated with silver paint on to the frame.

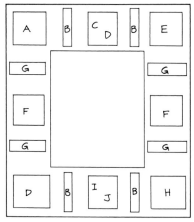

FLOWER KEY
A Love-in-a-mist B Snowdrop C Cow parsley D Senecio E Curry plant F Clematis G Daisy H Lichen moss I Gypsophila J Pansy

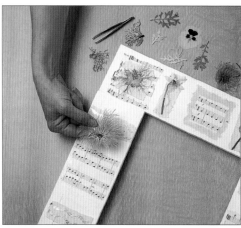

In this striking mirror frame, love-in-a-mist, curry plant, lichen moss, and pansies are mounted on to sheet music, while, in between, delicate lines of daisies are glued on to silver-painted paper.

4 Arrange silver and white pressed plant material on top of the larger pieces of paper, making sure the design is balanced, and glue in position. Next arrange three pressed daisies on to four of the smaller paper strips and pressed snowdrops on to the remaining four. Glue these on to the mirror frame.

5 Finally, apply a coat of clear water-based matt varnish over the entire frame. Use a soft paintbrush to apply the varnish and ensure that the pressed material is completely covered. Leave to dry and then apply a second coat.

FLORAL CALENDAR

In this floral calendar design I have tried to represent the seasonal changes in the flowering year. The picture is divided into twelve sections, each one numbered to correspond to the calendar months. Within each month, selected pressed flowers or foliage are mounted on to handmade papers. If you prefer, you could alter the design to include your favourite flowers.

YOU WILL NEED

Handmade papers

Ruler

Glue

Artist's watercolour paper

Pencil

Watercolour paints

Paintbrush

Eraser

Lavender stems

Calligraphy pen

Scissors

Pressed flowers

1 Gently tear the handmade paper into a rectangle measuring approximately 30 x 23cm (12 x 9¼in). Do not cut the handmade paper with scissors; the edges should look natural. Glue this paper down firmly in the centre of the watercolour paper. Next draw on the handmade paper the lines of the grid showing twelve squares, and add the lines for the floral border on the outer edge (see line drawing).

2 Using a fine paintbrush, apply an even watercolour wash over the border surround, keeping carefully within the pencil lines. A neutral colour wash works well for the border as this will not detract from the centre of the design, which will be multi-coloured. When the paint has dried thoroughly, gently erase all the outer border pencil lines.

3 Form the lines which divide the central twelve sections with lavender stems. Try to use long straight stems to cover the original pencil lines and glue in position. Tear twelve small pieces of handmade paper and glue these within each of the twelve squares.

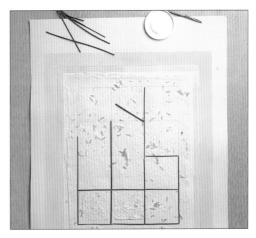

FLOWER KEY
A Snowdrop B Catkin C Primrose
D Forget-me-not E Pansy F Fuchsia
G Lavender H Delphinium I Tansy
J Tree of heaven K Heather L Holly
M Cow parsley N Lady's-mantle
O Hogweed P Rose foliage
Q Southernwood R Rose
S Lady's-bedstraw T Gypsophila

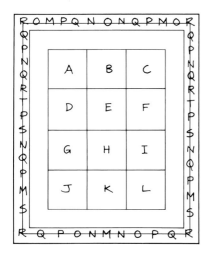

4 With a calligraphy pen, neatly write the numbers I to XII in Roman numerals on to watercolour paper. Cut out the numbers. When the ink is dry, glue the numbered squares on top of small pieces of textured brown paper in the calendar sections.

5 Select pressed flower that will fit within the calendar borders and arrange them on the design. When you are satisfied with the overall balance, glue the flowers in place. Decorate the surrounding border in the same way.

The first four months of this floral calendar are represented by the spring flowers of snowdrop, catkin, primrose and forget-me-not. For the summer months, pansy, fuchsia, lavender and delphinium are shown, while autumn and winter are represented by tansy, autumn leaves, heather and holly.

PAPIER MÂCHÉ BOWL

Papier mâché, the craft of modelling with paper pulp, has had a major revival in recent years. This bowl, standing on three ball feet, was moulded from an existing bowl and edged with a wide rim to allow plenty of scope for decorating. The bowl was first painted and stencilled before being decorated with pressed stocks, roses, philadelphus, cow parsley and delphiniums.

YOU WILL NEED

Papier mâché bowl

Paintbrush

Acrylic paint

Stencil brush

Diamond stencil

Paper towel

Pressed flowers

Glue

Water-based matt varnish

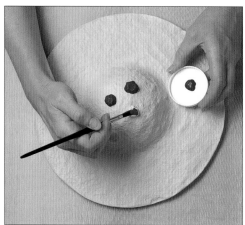

1 Paint the papier mâché bowl with cream acrylic paint. When dry, apply another coat to achieve an even paint tone over the entire bowl. Leave to dry. Paint the bowl's three ball feet with blue acrylic paint; several layers may be needed to complement the pressed delphiniums. Leave to dry.

2 Using blue acrylic paint, a stencil brush and a diamond stencil (see template on page 94), stencil a small border around the top edge of the inner bowl. Leave to dry.

3 Arrange cream and blue pressed flowers around the rim of the bowl to form a complete floral layer. When you are happy with the overall colour balance of the rim, glue the flowers in place and leave to dry.

4 Using a soft paintbrush, apply a thin coat of matt varnish over the bowl, especially around the rim, where the bowl is more likely to be touched. When dry, apply a second coat, then leave to dry.

WEDDING PHOTOGRAPH ALBUM

Pressing flowers from a bridal bouquet is a wonderful way of preserving such special sentimental blooms. This beautiful wedding album was decorated with cream roses, gypsophila, peach carnations, variegated ivy and cow parsley mounted on to peach and cream dupion silks, the actual fabric from the bride's and bridesmaid's wedding dresses.

YOU WILL NEED

Handmade papers

Photograph album

Scissors

Artist's watercolour paper

Samples of bride's and bridesmaid's dress fabrics

Glue

Pressed bouquet flowers and foliage

FLOWER KEY
A Rose B Gypsophila C Rose foliage
D Carnation E Cow parsley
F Variegated ivy

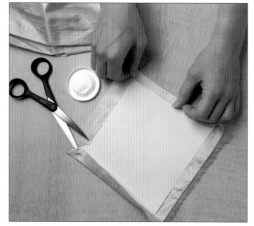

1 Tear a piece of handmade paper to a size to cover the front of the album. Cut an 18cm (7¹⁄₄in) square of watercolour paper and a 19cm (7¹⁄₂in) square of dress fabric. Glue the paper square on to the back of the fabric square. Glue the excess fabric on to the back of the paper square.

2 Cut an 8cm (3¹⁄₄in) square of watercolour paper and a 9cm (3¹⁄₂in) square of dress fabric and repeat step 1. When dry, glue the large square diagonally on to the centre of the handmade paper. Glue the smaller fabric square diagonally on the larger fabric square. Leave to dry.

3 Cut out four paper hearts and cover them with bridesmaid's dress fabric. Glue one fabric heart on to each corner of the handmade paper. Tear a heart shape out of handmade paper and glue in the central square.

4 Edge the central heart with pressed cow parsley and decorate the hearts with bridal roses. Glue a floral border on the larger square. Finally, glue the cover to the front of the photograph album.

WEDDING SAMPLER

Pressed bridal flowers have been used to create this pretty wedding sampler, which is based on the Victorian hobby of stitched samplers. These hand-sewn samplers usually commemorated a special occasion such as a wedding or a child's christening. Mounted and framed, this pressed flower wedding sampler can be kept as a personal reminder of a happy day.

YOU WILL NEED

Handmade papers

Ruler

Pencil

Scalpel and cutting board

Glue

Artist's watercolour paper

Scissors

Watercolour paint

Paintbrush

Eraser

Calligraphy pen

Pressed bridal flowers

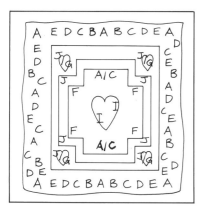

FLOWER KEY
A Rose (flowerhead) B Larkspur
C Gypsophila D Purple stock E Cream
stock F Hyacinth G Cow parsley H Rose
foliage I Rose petals J Rosebuds

1 Tear a rectangle of pink handmade paper measuring 30 x 24cm (12 x 9¹/₂in). Mark a line 4cm (1¹/₄in) in from the edge. Cut along this line. Glue the border on watercolour paper.

2 Tear a heart out of white handmade paper; glue in place. Cut a smaller heart from watercolour paper. Paint this pink; glue it on top. Paint a pink border around the central heart.

3 Using a calligraphy pen and black ink, write the names of the bride and groom on the heart, with the date of their marriage beneath. Practise on a piece of scrap paper first, for correct spacing. Cut four small heart shapes from red-toned pressed leaves, ensuring they are equal in size. Glue these on the four corners of the sampler.

4 Glue the pressed flowers on the pink border. Glue pressed pink rose petals around the central heart. Glue two pink roses and gypsophila above and below the heart, and four pink hyacinths on the inner corners of the border. Glue four small rosebuds on the border corners and soften the cut-out hearts with cow parsley.

WRITING PAPER

All stationery, from notelets and writing paper to gift tags and invitations, can be given a special, personal touch by the addition of pressed flowers. It can also be lightly perfumed by storing it in a sealed bag with a sachet of pot pourri for a few days. When decorating writing paper, choose a good quality handmade paper with a hard finish; soft paper absorbs too much moisture from the glue and buckles. These two writing papers have been designed to show how very different effects can easily be created. The white spring paper is decorated with delicate snowdrops, narcissi, catkins and lily-of-the-valley, with corresponding envelopes. A bold vertical line of pressed vegetables decorates the textured brown paper and would be suitable for both male and female correspondence. By experimenting with various shapes and positions of pressed material, writing paper can be bold and individual, limited only by your own imagination.

YOU WILL NEED

Pressed plant material

Handmade writing paper and envelopes

Glue

Water-based matt varnish

TIP
If you are planning to make your writing paper into a gift, it can be lovely to perfume it first. To add fragrance to the writing paper, place it in a cellophane bag along with a sachet of sweetly scented pot pourri. Tie the bag to seal in the contents and leave the paper for several days to absorb the perfume. Then you can simply include the pot pourri sachet with the writing paper gift.

SPRING PAPER
1 Lay the pressed snowdrops on to the bottom left-hand corner of the white handmade paper. Overlay these with pressed lily-of-the-valley, narcissi and catkins, radiating the stems from one point. Glue in position. Remember to glue the pressed material to the corner and edges of the paper, to ensure that there is enough room on the paper for actual letter writing. Then glue two snowdrops and their foliage to the top right-hand corner of the paper.

2 Using tweezers, place a small spray of flowers on the bottom left-hand corner of the envelope and glue in place. When dry, coat the pressed material with matt varnish to seal it to the paper.

VEGETABLE PAPER
Follow the same procedure to decorate brown handmade paper using a combination of pressed beetroot, carrot and spring onion. Decorate the envelope with a small pressed carrot and tomato.

GIFT WRAPPING PAPER

There is such a wonderful selection of ribbons, twines and papers widely available that gift wrapping can be highly individual and creative. These gift wrappings incorporate pressed herbs and foliage. Brown paper is revamped with the addition of pressed autumn leaves, while the herb paper has a more delicate appearance, with the names of the pressed herbs printed in Latin.

YOU WILL NEED

Brown paper

Sticky tape

Gold pen

Handmade papers

Glue

Pressed autumn foliage

Ribbon

Soft brown pencil

Ruler

Pressed herbs

AUTUMN LEAF WRAPPING PAPER

1 Wrap the present in brown paper. Using a gold pen, decorate the entire present with designs of small gold stars and circles. Leave to dry.

2 Tear squares of natural handmade paper and dark green handmade paper. Glue these over the wrapped present, placing the green paper on top of the natural paper. Glue autumn leaves on top. Finish with a bow.

HERB WRAPPING PAPER

1 Lay a sheet of natural handmade paper down flat. Using a soft dark pencil and ruler, lightly draw criss-crossing diagonal lines over the paper to make diamond shapes.

2 Glue sprigs of pressed herbs in the diamond shapes on the paper, alternating the herbs so that no two adjacent sections are the same. Then write the Latin name of the herb on the edge of each section, using the soft pencil. Wrap up the parcel and tie a bow around it to complete.

CHRISTMAS CARDS

Christmas is the season of goodwill and the time we exchange our good wishes of peace and hope to one another by sending greetings cards. These four designs show how pressed flowers and foliage can be used to make attractive and individual cards. By incorporating textured paper, hessian, tartan ribbons and twines, many variations can be achieved.

YOU WILL NEED

Scissors

Ruler

Handmade papers

Artist's watercolour paper

Glue

Hessian

Tartan ribbons

Pressed foliage, flowers and fruit

Twine and cord

Sponge

Gold paint

Paintbrush

Gold ribbon

ORANGE AND CINNAMON CARD

1 Cut a rectangle 22 x 15cm (9 x 6in) from handmade paper. Fold it in half to make a card 11 x 15cm (4³/₈ x 6in). Cut a rectangle measuring 21 x 14cm (8³/₈ x 5¹/₂in) from watercolour paper; fold as before. Glue this to the inside of the handmade paper card.

2 Cut a square of hessian leaving frayed edges; glue this on the green card. Cut a smaller square of green tartan ribbon; glue this on the hessian. Glue a large fern diagonally across the ribbon, then add an orange slice in the centre. Knot green twine around two cinnamon sticks; glue to the orange.

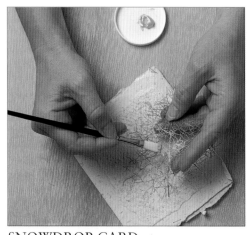

SNOWDROP CARD

1 Tear a square from white handmade paper and sponge it gold. Glue it to the white card. Brush gold paint over pressed fennel, leave to dry, then glue it on the gold card.

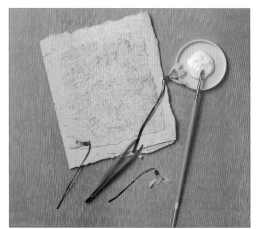

2 Arrange seven pressed snowdrops with foliage on to the card, so that they all radiate from the same point. Glue into place. Tie a gold ribbon in a small bow and glue this on the point from where the snowdrops radiate.

Orange and cinnamon card

Snowdrop card

Tartan heart card

Christmas pudding card

TARTAN HEART CARD

1 Tear a square of natural-toned handmade paper to fit on to the front of a basic red card and glue into place. Tear two squares of green paper and place one on the top left-hand corner and one on the bottom right-hand corner of the natural handmade paper. Glue in place.

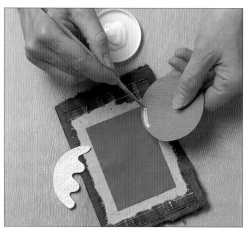

CHRISTMAS PUDDING CARD

1 Cut a rectangle of red tartan to fit on to the front of a green card and glue in place. Tear a slightly smaller rectangle of natural paper and glue this on to the tartan. Cut a small rectangle of red paper and glue it on the centre of the card. Place a circle of brown paper on to the card and glue in position.

2 Cut two small red tartan hearts and two green tartan hearts and stick these on to the four paper quarters. Stick pressed holly leaves on to the two green hearts and pressed ivy leaves on to the red hearts. Glue green cord along the central line of the four squares and then two shorter pieces of cord to define the cross shape.

2 Make a semi-circle of white paper, the same circumference as the brown circle. Using scissors, cut a wavy line across the semi-circle to form the pudding's icing. Glue to the card. Paint four hogweed flowers with gold paint; when dry, stick these on to the four corners of the red card, then overlay them with pressed ivy leaves. Finally, glue a sprig of pressed holly and berries on the top of the Christmas pudding.

CHRISTMAS TREE DECORATIONS

In the exciting days before Christmas, it is always great fun to follow the tradition of decorating our homes, making them look special for the festive season. Central to these decorations is the Christmas tree. There are many styles of decorations for these trees, from traditional bells, baubles and candles to more contemporary designs. These pressed flower and foliage decorations have been made from heart and star shapes, cut from medium density fibreboard (MDF). Silver-painted holly is backed by textured papers, grey foliage and silver wires, while green pressed ivy, lily-of-the-valley and hogweed create a decoration in a more traditional style. These Christmas decorations will be treasured by you and your family for years to come.

YOU WILL NEED

MDF hearts and stars

Emulsion paint

Sponge

Paintbrush

Glue

Handmade paper

Silver florist wire

Pressed flowers and foliage

Ribbon

POPPY STAR

1 Paint the MDF star all over with white paint. When dry, apply a second coat of paint. Select a textured white paper and tear it into a star shape, to fit on to the front of the decoration. Glue the paper on to the star and leave to dry.

2 Glue a pressed senecio leaf on to the textured paper star. Bend lengths of silver florist wire into interesting swirly and zigzag shapes and then lay these on the star so that they overhang the edges. Next glue a large silver-painted holly leaf on top of the wires to hold them in position. Slice a poppy seedhead in half and glue it on top of the holly leaf, cut side down. Finally, to complete the decoration, tie a silver ribbon bow to the top of the star, and leave a hoop to hang the star from the tree.

Poppy star tree decoration

Ivy leaf heart

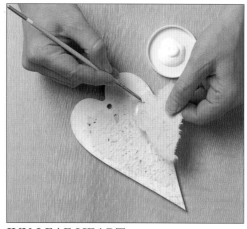

IVY LEAF HEART

1 Paint the MDF heart with white paint and leave to dry. Lightly sponge over this with gold paint to give a soft golden effect. Tear a piece of natural textured paper into a heart shape and glue this to the centre of the decoration. Then tear a smaller heart from a darker-toned paper and glue this on to the first paper heart. Leave to dry.

2 Using gold paint and a paintbrush, paint the pressed spiky foliage of monkshood and two small hydrangea heads. When dry, glue the gold monkshood leaves on to the heart. Next, glue three pressed green ivy leaves down the centre of the decoration, graduating the size of leaf towards the bottom. Glue the two gold-painted hydrangea leaves on top of the ivy and finish the decoration with a gold string.

SILVER FENNEL STAR

Paint the star all over with two coats of white paint. When dry, glue a large spray of pressed fennel on to the star. Then glue the layers of pressed material on top of each other in the centre of the star, first silver senecio, then three silver-painted holly leaves and finally a pressed clematis seedhead. Finish the decoration with a silver ribbon bow.

DARK GREEN HEART

Paint the MDF heart with green emulsion; when dry, glue a heart shape of coarse hessian to the front of the heart. Then glue a small heart of natural, textured paper on to this and overlay it with a green pressed fern and a sprig of pressed fennel. Paint two stems of lily-of-the-valley and a hogweed flower gold; when dry, glue these on to the decoration and finish with a gold string.

PLANT COLOUR CHARTS

PINK/PEACH

Name of Plant	Pressing Method	When to Collect	Pressed Colour	Special Comment
Alstroemeria	Microwave or press with heat	Summer, all year from florist	Mid pink or scarlet	
Aquilegia	Traditional press	Early summer	Strong purple	
Astilbe	Traditional press	Summer	Pale pink	Thin sprays before pressing
Bougainvillea	Traditional press	Bracts in summer	Dark pink/mauve	Press individual bracts
Campion, red	Traditional press	Spring – autumn	Rose pink	
Carnation, pink	Press with heat	Mid summer, all year from florist	Pale pink	Dismantle flower, press, then reassemble
Cherry blossom	Traditional press	Late winter – early summer	Light pink	Press individual flowers
Chive flower	Press with heat	Flowers in summer	Deep pink	
Chrysanthemum, pink daisy	Microwave	All year from florist	Mid pink	Press individual flowers full face
Clematis, pink	Traditional press	Spring – early autumn	Mid pink	
Cosmos	Traditional press	Summer – early autumn	Mid pink	
Cyclamen	Traditional press	Winter – spring	Dark pink	Remove stem, press in profile
Deutzia	Traditional press	Late spring – summer	Light pink	Press individual flowers full face
Diascia	Traditional press	Summer	Deep salmon pink	Thin sprays before pressing
Dicentra	Traditional press or press with heat	Spring – summer	Pink, white inner petals	Press individual flowers
Dog rose	Traditional press	Mid summer	Mid pink	Press full face
Foxglove	Traditional press	Summer	Pale/deep pink, speckled purple	Press individual flowers
Geranium, pink	Traditional press	Early summer – autumn	Bright pink	
Heather	Traditional press	Late summer – autumn	Deep pink	Individual flowers good for edging
Japanese anemone	Press with heat	Late summer – early autumn	Light pink	Remove stem, press full face
Larkspur	Traditional press	Mid summer	Strong pink	Press individual flowers or thinned flower spikes
Lupin, pink	Traditional press	Early summer	Mid pink	Press individual flowers, useful for edging
Marjoram	Traditional press	All summer	Mid pink	Thin out leaves and flowers before pressing
Penstemon	Traditional press	Early summer – autumn	Pink/purple	Press in profile
Phlox	Traditional press	Mid – late summer	Light pink	Press full face
Pink	Traditional press or press with heat	Summer	Mid pink	Press flowers when fully open

GREEN

Name of Plant	Pressing Method	When to Collect	Pressed Colour	Special Comment
Ash	Traditional press	Leaves spring – autumn	Light – mid green	Can be skeletonized
Asparagus fern	Microwave or traditional press	All year from florist	Mid green	
Astrantia	Traditional press	Summer – autumn	Light green, with hint of pink	Press individual flowers
Barley	Traditional press or iron	Summer	Light green	Presses quickly
Carrot leaf	Traditional press	Summer	Dark green	Thin out leaves before pressing
Chilli	Traditional press	All year in supermarket	Strong green	Slice in half lengthways before pressing
Euphorbia	Traditional press	Spring – summer	Strong green/ yellow bracts	Sap may irritate skin
Fern	Traditional press	Spring – autumn, some evergreen	Dark green	Presses quickly
Fritillaria	Traditional press	Spring	Light green	Remove stem, press in profile
Grasses	Traditional press or iron	Early – late summer	Range of greens	Presses quickly, can be ironed
Hacquetia	Traditional press	Late winter – late spring	Strong green, yellow eye	Remove stem, press full face
Hellebore	Traditional press	Late winter – early spring	Mid green	Remove seed pod before pressing
Hop	Traditional press	Autumn	Light green	Press bracts and leaves separately
Hydrangea	Traditional press	Late summer – mid autumn	Light green	Press individual flowers full face
Ivy	Traditional press	Leaves all year, autumn flowers	Dark green	Press leaves and stems separately
Kiwi fruit	Microwave	All year in supermarket	Mid green, black seeds	Slice thinly
Lavender stems	Traditional press	Late summer	Dark green	Ideal for edging
Maple	Traditional press or iron	Leaves spring – autumn	Mid green	Can be skeletonized
Mint	Traditional press	Leaves spring – autumn	Mid green	Thin out leaves before pressing
Moluccella	Traditional press	Summer	Light green	Press calyx full face
Moss	Traditional press	All year	Dark green	Remove all mud, needs minimum pressing
Nettle	Traditional press	Leaves spring – autumn	Mid green leaf, cream flower	Thin out leaves before pressing
Nicotiana	Traditional press	Late summer – autumn	Mid green flowers	
Oak	Traditional press or iron	Leaves spring – autumn	Yellow/green	Can be skeletonized
Parsley	Traditional press or press with heat	Summer, all year from supermarket	Dark green	Press when young
Pear	Microwave	Autumn, all year from supermarket	Light green	Slice thinly
Rosemary	Traditional press	Leaves all year	Grey green	Silver underside
Runner bean	Traditional press	Summer	Dark green	Press young
Sycamore	Traditional press or iron	Leaves spring – autumn	Mid green	Can be skeletonized
Thistle leaf	Traditional press or press with heat	Spring – autumn	Dark green	Press young leaves, silver underside

BROWN/RED

Name of Plant	Pressing Method	When to Collect	Pressed Colour	Special Comment
Acer	Traditional press	Autumn	Red or purple	
Anemone	Traditional press or press with heat	Spring – early summer	Bright red to purple	Remove stem, press full face
Antirrhinum	Traditional press	Spring – autumn	Dark red	Press individual flowers
Apple	Microwave	Autumn, all year from supermarket	Red/green	Slice thinly
Bark	Traditional press	All year	Dark brown	Minimum pressure required
Blackberry	Traditional press or press with heat	Late summer	Black or red	Thin out spray, press before ripe
Bracken	Traditional press or iron	Autumn	Mid brown	
Bronze fennel	Traditional press	Summer	Brown	Useful for backgrounds
Catkin	Traditional press	Late winter – early spring	Brownish-green or yellow	
Chilli	Traditional press	Summer, all year from supermarket	Strong red	Slice lengthways before pressing
Crocosmia	Traditional press	Late summer	Strong red	Remove flowers from stem
Field poppy	Traditional press	Summer	Dark red	Remove stem, press full face
Fuchsia	Traditional press	Early summer – early autumn	Dark red and purple	Use small hardy varieties only
Geranium, annual	Traditional press	Early summer – autumn	Strong, bright red	Press individual flowers
Holly	Traditional press	Berries in autumn	Dark brown	Press young leaves when soft
Honeysuckle	Traditional press	Summer – early autumn	Dark red	Press just before flower fully open
Hydrangea	Traditional press	Late summer – mid autumn	Dark red or purple	Press individual flowers full face
Lady's-bedstraw	Traditional press	Mid – late summer	Rust brown	Thin spray before pressing
Mushroom/fungi	Traditional press	Autumn	Brown or beige	Press small fungi whole, slice large ones in half
Plantain	Traditional press	Late spring – autumn	Dark brown	Stems useful for edging
Rose hips	Traditional press	Autumn	Red or orange	Slice in half, remove soft pulp, pad with tissue
Rose, red	Press with heat	Summer, all year from florist	Deep red	Slice in half before pressing
Salvia	Traditional press	Late summer – autumn	Bright red	
Seaweed	Traditional press	All year	Brown, cream or green	Wash salt off, then press
Skeletonized leaves	Traditional press or iron	Autumn	Brown	Useful for backgrounds
Sorrel	Traditional press	Late summer – autumn	Dark red	Thin sprays for pressing
Strawberry	Traditional press	Summer, extended season in supermarket	Bright red	Slice in half, remove soft pulp, pad with tissue
Tomato	Microwave	Summer, all year from supermarket	Mid red	Cut in half or slice thinly
Virginia creeper	Traditional press	Leaves in autumn	Rich red	Press individual leaves
Walnut leaf	Traditional press	Spring – early summer	Dark brown	Use young leaves

YELLOW/ORANGE/CREAM

Name of Plant	Pressing Method	When to Collect	Pressed Colour	Special Comment
Achillea	Traditional press	Summer	Deep yellow	Remove stem, press florets
Aconite	Traditional press	Late winter – early spring	Mid yellow	Press full face
Agrimony	Traditional press	Summer	Light yellow	Press whole spike
Antirrhinum	Traditional press	Summer	Mid yellow	Press individual flowers
Bird's-foot trefoil	Traditional press	Summer	Mid yellow, tinged red	
Buttercup	Traditional press	Spring – summer	Strong yellow	Remove stem, press full face
Carrot	Traditional press or press with heat	Summer – early autumn	Mid orange	Cut in half or thin slices
Carrot flower	Traditional press	Summer	Warm cream	Remove stem, press full face
Celandine	Traditional press	Spring – summer	Bright yellow	Remove stem, press full face
Chrysanthemum, yellow daisy	Microwave	All year from florist	Mid yellow	Press individual flowers full face
Cowslip	Press with heat	Spring	Strong yellow	Remove flowers, press and rebuild
Crocosmia	Traditional press	Summer	Strong orange	Remove flowers from stem
Daffodil	Traditional press or press with heat	Late spring	Light yellow	Remove trumpet, press and rebuild
Doronicum	Traditional press	Late spring	Strong yellow	Remove stem, press full face
Forsythia	Traditional press	Spring	Bright yellow	Press flowers, remove stem
Hogweed	Traditional press	Summer	Cream	Press individual florets full face
Honeysuckle	Traditional press	Summer	Cream/yellow	Press just before fully open
Laburnum	Traditional press	Late spring	Light yellow	Thin sprays, press whole
Lady's-mantle	Traditional press	Summer	Yellow/green	Thin sprays before pressing
Lily, yellow, orange, cream	Traditional press or press with heat	Summer, all year from florist	Deep yellow, orange, cream	Remove petals, press, reassemble when pressed
Loosestrife	Traditional press	Summer	Bright yellow	Press flowers full face
Lupin, yellow	Traditional press	Early summer	Mid yellow	Press flowers, good for edging
Mimosa	Traditional press	Spring, from florist	Bright yellow	Thin out spikes before pressing
Nasturtium	Traditional press	Mid summer – autumn	Strong orange	Press in profile
Pansy	Traditional press	Spring – summer	Bright yellow, brown centre	Remove stem, press full face
Primrose	Traditional press	Spring	Fresh yellow	Press flowers full face
Rose, yellow	Press with heat	Summer, all year from florist	Mid yellow	Cut in half before pressing
Solidago	Traditional press	Late summer – early autumn	Dark yellow	Thin out flowers before pressing
Stock, cream	Press with heat	Summer, longer from florist	Rich cream	Thin petals, press flowers full face
Tulip, yellow	Microwave	Spring	Mid yellow	Press petals
Wallflower	Traditional press	Spring – summer	Strong yellow/orange	

WHITE/SILVER

Name of Plant	Pressing Method	When to Collect	Pressed Colour	Special Comment
Alyssum	Traditional press	Summer	Clean white	
Artemisia	Traditional press	Leaves spring – autumn	Silvery white	
Cineraria	Traditional press	Leaves all year	Silvery grey	Press individual leaves
Clover	Traditional press	Summer	Creamy white	
Cow parsley	Traditional press	Early summer	Creamy white	Press entire flower
Crambe	Traditional press	Mid – late summer	White	Press in small sprays
Daisy, garden	Traditional press	All summer	White with yellow centre	Remove stems, press full face
Deutzia	Traditional press	Late spring – summer	Creamy white	Thin flower sprays before pressing
Gypsophila	Traditional press	All year from florist	Soft creamy white	Press in small sprays
Heather	Traditional press	Late summer – autumn	White	
Larkspur	Traditional press	Mid summer	Clean white	Press individual flowers or thinned flower spikes
Lichen moss	Traditional press	Winter – spring	Silvery grey	
Lily-of-the-valley	Microwave then press with heat	Late spring	Creamy white	$3/4$ power for 1 min, finish with heated press
Lily, white	Traditional press or with heat	Summer, all year from florist	Creamy white	Remove petals, press, then reassemble
Love-in-a-mist	Traditional press	Summer	White	Press full face
Marguerite daisy	Traditional press	Summer	White with yellow centre	Press full face
Onion	Traditional press	Summer	Creamy white	Slice small onions in half or thin cross sections
Orchid	Microwave	All year from florist	White	Remove centre tongue, 1 min on $3/4$ power
Phlox	Traditional press	Summer	Creamy white	Press full face
Pulsatilla seedhead	Traditional press	Late spring	Silvery grey	
Rose, white	Press with heat	Summer	Creamy white	Cut flowers in half before pressing
Rue	Traditional press	Leaves all year	Silvery grey	
Sage foliage	Traditional press	Leaves all year	Silvery grey	Press individual leaves
Santolina foliage	Traditional press	Leaves all year	Silvery grey	
Snowdrop	Traditional press	Late winter – Early spring	White/green	Remove leaves, press with stem
Star-of-Bethlehem	Traditional press	Early summer	White/green	Remove stem and press full face
Stephanotis	Microwave	Early summer – autumn	White	Remove calyx and shank, press full face
Traveller's joy	Traditional press	Seedheads in autumn	Silvery grey	
Whitebeam	Traditional press	Spring – autumn	Silvery white	Press individual leaves
Willow, pussy	Traditional press	Leaves spring – autumn	Dark grey	Press on stem

BLUE/PURPLE

Name of Plant	Pressing Method	When to Collect	Pressed Colour	Special Comment
African violet	Traditional press	All year on indoor plants	Rich purple	Remove stems, leaves, press full face
Allium	Traditional press	Early summer	Deep purple	Press individual flowerheads
Anemone	Traditional press or press with heat	Spring – early summer	Rich blue or purple	Remove stem and press full face
Aquilegia	Traditional press	Early summer	Strong purple	
Berberis leaf	Traditional press	Autumn	Reddish-purple	Remove stems and thorns
Bluebell	Traditional press or press with heat	Spring	Dark blue	Remove flowers, then rebuild
Borage	Traditional press	Summer	Strong blue	Remove calyx, press flowers
Campanula	Traditional press	Mid summer	Light blue	Difficult to press
Ceanothus	Traditional press	Late spring – autumn	Dark blue	Separate into sprays
Cornflower	Traditional press	Summer – early autumn	Rich blue	Remove calyx, press full face
Delphinium	Traditional press	Summer	Strong range of blues	Press individual flowers
Forget-me-not	Traditional press	Early summer	Sky blue	Press in sprays
Freesia	Microwave	All year from florist	Deep purple	Separate petals and press
Geranium, perennial	Traditional press	Early summer – autumn	Blue/purple	Press full face
Honesty	Traditional press	Spring – early summer	Deep purple	
Hyacinth	Traditional press	Spring	Dark blue	Slice flowers in half lengthways
Iris	Press with heat	Late spring – summer	Dark blue with yellow centre	Press petals, then reconstruct
Larkspur	Traditional press	Summer	Strong purple	Press full face or thinned spikes
Lavender	Traditional press	Mid – late summer	Dark blue or silver blue	
Lilac	Microwave	Late spring	Pale mauve	Press small groups of florets
Lobelia	Traditional press	Summer – early autumn	Dark blue	Thin out sprays before pressing
Love-in-a-mist	Traditional press	Summer	Sky blue	Press full face
Monkshood	Traditional press	Mid summer	Dark blue	Press flowers and young spikes
Muscari	Press with heat	Spring	Dark, rich blue	
Pansy	Traditional press	Spring – summer	Rich blue	Remove stem, press full face
Penstemon	Traditional press	Early summer – autumn	Dark purple	Press in profile
Periwinkle	Traditional press	Late spring – early autumn	Dark blue	Remove calyx, press full face
Primula	Traditional press	Spring	Dark purple	Remove calyx before pressing
Scabious	Traditional press or press with heat	Summer	Light blue	Remove stem and press full face
Statice	Traditional press	Summer – autumn	Blue or purple	Presses easily
Stock	Press with heat	Summer, longer from florist	Light purple	Press full face
Veronica	Traditional press	Summer – early autumn	Mid blue	Remove excess foliage
Viola	Traditional press	Spring – summer	Rich purple	Remove stem and press full face

Stencil Templates

A Spring Wooden Trug (page 34)
B & C Seaside Photo Frame (page 42)
D Wooden Tray (page 60)
E Papier Mâché Bowl (page 72)

INDEX

SUPPLIERS

Picture framing and mounts Careys
Picture Framers, 12 Castle Close,
Wing, Leighton Buzzard,
Bedfordshire LU7 0TD;
Telephone: 01296 681969

Wooden tray Debenhams
Department Store

Hat box The Decorative Arts
Company Ltd, 5a Royal Crescent,
London W11 4SN
Telephone: 0171-371 4303

Shaker box Shaker, 25 Harcourt
Street, London W1H 1DT;
Telephone 0171-724 7672
Fax: 0171-724 6640

Terracotta pot Bressingham Plant
Centre, Dorney Court, Slough;
Telephone: 01628 669999

Candle Hand Carved Candle Co,
1 Foundry House, Hall Street,
Long Melford, Sudbury, Suffolk
CO10 9JB
Telephone/Fax: 01787 313342

Wooden trug Nature's Glory Ltd,
75 London Road, St Albans,
Hertfordshire AL1 1LN
Telephone: 01727 858582

**Papier mâché bowl and photograph
album** Sara Green, 60 Tye Green,
Glemsford, Sudbury, Suffolk
CO10 7RG
Telephone: 01787 280096

**MDF products, stencils, paints and
varnish** Paper and Paint Effects,
17 Hollywell Hill, St Albans,
Hertfordshire AL1 1EX
Telephone: 01727 836338

ACKNOWLEDGEMENTS

The author would like to thank the
following for their assistance with
New Pressed Flower Designs :

the commissioning editor Karen
Hemingway for her assistance; the
editor Heather Dewhurst; the
designer Sara Kidd; the
photographer Caroline Arber for her
beautiful photography; the stylist
Jane Cudlipp for the use of her
lovely home; Lorna Wareham and
Jean Morris for the generosity of
their gardens; and, lastly, special
thanks to Ian Morris.

For details of the work of Alison
Morris, please write to:

Under Pressure
Fishers Cottage
Fenstead End
Boxted
Bury St Edmunds
Suffolk IP29 4LH